To Sunny!
God Bless!
Stay Strong!
Never give up!

WHY JERMAINE?

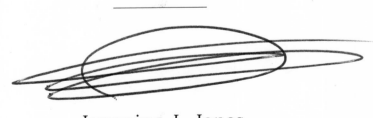

Jermaine J. Jones

10/14/2020

WHY JERMAINE?

ISBN 978-0-578-74087-4

Cover design: Matt Falkenstein

Website: whyjermaine.com
Email: jermaine@whyjermaine.com
Social Media: @WhyJermaine_book (IG)
          @JermaineWhy (Twitter)

Disclaimer

This book is dedicated to my beautiful mother, Helen Anita Jones, and my late father, Robert Lee Chambliss Jr. For years, my mother would say she wished she could have given her kids a better life. So, this is me giving my mother her flowers while she can still smell them.

Thank you Mother!

Acknowledgements

THANK YOU to all of the contributors to the Why Jermaine? Project. Your sacrifice of time is greatly appreciated, but more importantly, thank you for your genuine friendship! (Listed in Alphabetical Order by Last Name):

Faith Alcantara

Dave Amerson

Darlene Anderson

Marjory E. Avant Esq.

Sherwin L. Bentick

Eden Fowler Benton

John F. Berry Jr.

Kathie Britto

Bruce Broussard

Aleia K. Brown

Sgt. Manuel A. Cancel II

Chad Cisneros

Shareef Cleveland

Diann Coles

Michael Currington

Robert Davis

Det. C. Brooks

Larry Drexler

Dawn Monique Edmond

Renee Evelyn

Jason Falchuk

Matt Falkenstein

Sean Feeney

Najah Ford

Emily Gafanhao

Ariel Givens

Nicole Graves-Watson

Brenda Green

Timothy Greene

Drew Grisham

Darold Hall

Garrett Harker

Lailah Harrigan

Tashfia Hasan

David Herndon

Jermaine Hill

Dan Hogan

Tara Horniacek

Anjinette Hudson

Annie Jimenez

Christopher Knighton

Joseph J. Kranz

Jeannette Laguna

Appolos Laurient

Robert Lorenzo

Susanne Mancheno

Onique McFarlane

Robin Miller

Aysh-sha Morgano

Tim Murphy

Kelsey Oliveira

Melanie Oliveira

Zelia Oliveira

Neil Padden

Ty Page

Susan Pope

Amy Pozmantier

Alyssa Radigan

Eric Rhett

Sue Sedivec

Ron Shaich

Noah Siegel

Capt. Robert Smith

Kenny E. Spinks

Rebecca Stein

Robert Sullivan

Chris Taylor

Thomas & Michelle Taylor

Denise Tolbert

Teresa Tolbert

Laura Toni-Holsinger

Wil Townsend

Karen Trais

Sylvia Veitia

Brenda Walker

Ibn Wallace

Bobby Williams

Tyrone Williams Jr.

Tom Worstell

Steven J. Young

Foreword

It is with great privilege, and pressure, that I am a part of this journey called *Why Jermaine*. This book has inspired me to reflect on the lessons I have learned from Jermaine as we've traveled across New Jersey serving hot meals to those in need, and crisscrossed the country for speaking events in front of thousands. These lessons could write a book entirely their own, but I have learned that many of the lessons were learned on the day I met Jermaine – with the number one lesson being *consistency*. From summer camp at The Salvation Army in Newark to the stage of the Grand Ole Opry in front of thousands for Panera Bread, Jermaine is consistent. After all, "Consistency is Key".

I will never forget the day that I met Jermaine J. Jones. At the ripe old age of 30, I found myself in a discouraged and cynical state of mind without much of an idea for where life was going. Through a mutual colleague, Jermaine was invited to be a guest speaker for the summer day camp that I was managing in the summer of 2015. It was a challenging summer, to say the least. Jermaine bounced through the steel doors about an hour before he was scheduled to speak announcing, "Good morning! I'm here for the career day! I'm here to talk to the kids!" Four weeks into a six week summer camp, all the staff could think about was counting down the hours to the finish line. I'm ashamed to say that Jermaine received far less than an inviting welcome. As I recall, my exact words to him were "Good morning, you can sit in here until we're ready to start," pointing to our poor excuse for a conference room which served more as a storage closet. Years later I would learn that Jermaine did not get offended by this "warm" welcome but used it as a way to craft his message that day. Little did I know, that what I thought would be a one-off encounter with Jermaine would grow into a business relationship, journeys together across states, speaking events for thousands in the audience, and more importantly, a lifelong friendship.

As can be seen throughout *Why Jermaine*, Jermaine has an unmatched ability to captivate an audience. Reflecting back on that day in August 2015 one thing that stands out to me is how quiet the room was when Jermaine spoke with our group of 6-12 year old balls of energy. The summer was an ongoing battle of working to get the children to listen when someone was speaking. From the moment Jermaine stood up, he had eyes locked on him, darting back and forth as he worked the room to ensure he engaged each and every person. Later, I would have the same privilege of witnessing Jermaine engage a room of 300+ employees at Barclays in Wilmington, DE where a hush fell over the audience as Jermaine delivered the exact message needed for the audience. Even later, when Jermaine delivered the Keynote for the Black Achievers, I would witness the eyes of the Mayor of Wilmington, DE dart back and forth, following Jermaine's words in the same way the young campers' eyes did. It was there that Jermaine, and Mama Jones, received the Mayor's first ever distributed Key to the City. After the event we learned that the Mayor almost never stayed for the entirety of an event. As I continued to work with Jermaine I learned that he has an amazing ability to craft his message for the audience. I learned that he is literally building his message for the audience through every interaction, from the start of organizing an event up to the moments before he steps on the stage where he reads the room and finds exactly who needs to hear his message. It is one of the most empowering things that I have ever witnessed.

Jermaine delivered a powerful message to our campers that day in 2015, sharing intimate stories of his challenges growing up around the corner in the very same rough neighborhood where he was speaking to the campers to losing his job and contemplating taking his life. As we reflected together on his message, I shared how this young lady or that young man really needed the message because they were going through some great challenges. He looked at me with great confidence and sincerity and said, "I know." He intentionally engaged those very children because he could feel their pain and struggles. Years later, I would be blown away when Jermaine and I took a long, winding journey to Louisville, KY to speak to an audience of – surprising to us – mostly seniors of a mentoring program. As Jermaine worked the room before the event began, he was taking mental notes. With each 'good morning,' he was putting the final touches on what that day's message. In the dozens and dozens of times I've heard Jermaine speak to an audience each and every message has been unique. This message was unlike any other, but still held true and was timely. After the event, as he does with so many others, Jermaine took time to speak to everyone who came up to him. My jaw dropped when a woman in her sixties came up to Jermaine and said, "thank you, you've changed my life!" These same words would be shared by students at career days and executive leaders of businesses throughout the country.

I could go on and on reflecting on the journeys from New Jersey to Florida, to Virginia, to Massachusetts, and back again. However, as a reader you need to experience these journeys in the words of those that have believed in, been inspired by, and had their lives changed by their encounters with Jermaine. From student, to mentee, to entrepreneur, *Why Jermaine* shares lessons learned, impact made, and offers a glimpse of the wild journey of a man who has one mission – to change just one person's life.

Thank you Jermaine, my mentor, my business partner, and friend. Thank you for the honor of sharing in your journey, for changing my life, and allowing me to learn from you.

To the readers, I hope I have done justice in giving you a glimpse of the impact Jermaine has had on thousands of lives. As he traveled to speak to an audience of quite literally two or two thousand, one thing held true...consistency. "Why Jermaine?" because he is consistent, genuine, and his journey speaks to everyone from the Janitor to the CEO.

Drew Grisham

WHY JERMAINE?
TABLE OF CONTRIBUTORS

Why Jermaine?

Dave Amerson

President, NeoTract Interventional Urology &
Teleflex

"Perpetual optimism is a force multiplier," Colin Powell. Jermaine lives by this motto and has positively impacted so many with his positive actions. I met Jermaine in January 2015 at Penn Station in NYC. The station was jam-packed with holiday travelers as me, my wife (Lori) and daughter (Kendall) were heading on Amtrak to Washington, DC to see family. Kendall, who suffers from anxiety, passes out while waiting in line to board our train. There we are in crowded Penn Station, with our daughter lying on the ground, not knowing what to do next. Then comes our Angel, Jermaine Jones. Jermaine immediately grabbed a wheelchair and took us to the Amtrak lounge for Kendall to recover, booked us on the next train to DC, and made sure we were safe & sound. I can never thank Jermaine enough for being an example of steward leadership. Steward leaders adopt a "we" perspective instead of an "I" perspective. Jermaine's leadership encourages others to go beyond the normal.

Jermaine is also making a significant contribution in his community through Brothers Making a Difference. Thanks Jermaine, for making a difference in our lives, and others, every day!

Why Jermaine?

Kathie Britto

Reflecting back, I can't recall my very first encounter with Jermaine. He's one of those rare people who I feel I've known my whole life, though I know that's not possible I will say, from the beginning to present, seeing him is always such a pleasant, high energy and joyful experience. He's one of those 'old souls' who is full of wisdom & knowledge. He somehow in any situation, always knows the right things to say. I can be having the worst day, and being greeted with that big smile & genuine hug always kind of helps me put things in perspective.

As the years have gone on, and my friendship with Jermaine grew, I've learned of his organization, Brothers making a Difference. I thought, what a perfect name. This brother, in a short time, has made a difference in my day, many days by being such a positive, caring friend with the ability to not only listen, but to actually hear and comprehend my concerns. What I think he's so gifted at is not necessarily having answers to everything you present to him, but having the ability to give another perspective, where I'm asking myself other questions and broadening my thought process.

I truly believe that his gift is a blessing from a higher power, and one that he has found a way to share with others. He is making a difference; he understands that one life at a time is so important. He is one of the most giving people I know & I'm sure many who know him will agree. His positivity is contagious. He remains the same humble man I met years ago, and his joy is to spread what others have done. Anyone seeking to follow his path would be wise to maintain those core values.

I often think how different life could have been for not only myself, but especially my sons and nephews, had they had this type of program; more importantly, the type of man Jermaine is, to follow or have around to ask questions, seek guidance or just see philanthropy at its finest. When you give, you receive so much more.

Jermaine has been a constant, positive force in my life. He's one of those priceless friends that I know I'll have forever. We could go months without seeing each other, but if we ran into each other, it would be like no time has passed. In addition to the qualities I've mentioned, he's also very funny. A great sense of humor is needed in life, and he's definitely one to make you laugh. I feel we all cross paths for a reason, and many times the reason is unknown to us. With wisdom, I've learned the why isn't always important. I'm so grateful for the blessing. A friend who has dedicated himself to doing something daily to make the world a better place. A friend that greets you with a big smile and bigger hug. A friend who checks in, makes you laugh, makes you think and makes you better. That's Jermaine. My friend, I'm so excited to see what the world has in store for you, and what great things you will do in this world.

Why Jermaine?

Marjory E. Avant, Esq.

Jermaine and I met in the summer of 2012. I was introduced to him by a former client who I had counseled regarding the formation of a non-profit organization. Jermaine shared with me his interest in creating his own non-profit organization whose focus would be encouraging and motivating young people by organizing a one-to-one mentorship program similar to Big Brother/Sister. I strongly discouraged Jermaine from moving forward with this plan. He had a full-time job; a family; and no business experience. More specifically, he did not have a social work or education background; had no community-based organizing experience; and had never worked in the not-for- profit sector. My prior years of experience had demonstrated that zeal and interest did not equal success in a business endeavor – and a successful not-for-profit organization is run like a well-oiled machine. At that point in my career, I had encountered many people like Jermaine: they had identified a need and believed that their interest in addressing a social problem alone could overcome their shortcomings with business. I informed Jermaine that most of the non-profit organizations that I had formed had failed and were inactive within a few years after formation. I told him that the best intentions could not overcome the founders inexperience in identifying and motivating board members; founders did not know how to design and implement a fundraising plan; founders did not know who their competitors

7

were and what their competitors excelled at so that they could differentiate their service offerings; founders did not know how to identify and partner with the correct community partners to form joint ventures for collaboration and forming joint ventures. I told him the name of his organization was "stupid." I asked him, "Who wants to 'be mad'?" I was rudely condescending. I was arrogantly confident that the name alone was a repellent. I had become jaded by well-intentioned people's failure in the community service space. I didn't see Jermaine as an individual with an answer. Jermaine took umbrage with my observations and unequivocally told me that when he undertook an endeavor, his intention was to succeed at it. That was the moment my first impression of him took a 180-degree turn. Instantly, Jermaine became someone whose conviction to change the lives of young people through mentorship and encouragement was going to be realized. He possessed a winner's attitude and the laser-beam focus of a superstar.

Jermaine's driven spirit fueled my desire to help him accomplish his goal. Over the course of the next year we met several times. Our first meetings were focused on strategizing a plan for success for the non-profit "Brothers Making A Difference." Next, we documented those ideas in our communications with the IRS to advance the application submitted on behalf of Brothers Making A Difference to become a tax-exempt organization. Then, after the organization was awarded tax exempt status, we held a handful of board organization and responsibility training sessions with the people Jermaine had corralled into service.

The first year's activities with Jermaine of laying the foundation for Brother's Making a Difference's success proved that Jermaine was an outlier, easily distinguished from the previous individuals that I had met with for the same purpose(s) who only had a dream but lacked the calling that Jermaine had. Jermaine operated with the single-minded conviction of a man who had been called into battle.

Over the course of the past 8 years, Jermaine impressed me as a person who doesn't get stuck in "analysis paralysis" which prevents people from launching out of the starting block. As the years have passed, Jermaine's deep commitment to deliver his message of hope to the next generation of young people reached a fever pitch and the fruit of his labor was evident. The proclamations of the impact that he was having on people's lives were contained in the accolades he regularly received following an outing. I, too, became a believer that Jermaine Jones was the Real Deal; an effective mentor and motivator, encouraging and empowering young people to live their lives with hope and purpose. I identify myself as an overcomer and a person of accomplishment. Since this is how I view myself, I am drawn to people with the same energy. For that reason, it was easy to hitch my wagon to Jermaine. He has consistently exhibited an overcomer's mind set - no challenge too great; no obstacle that can't be scaled down to a manageable task. My energy and enthusiasm for the work Jermaine was doing is in direct response to his energy and enthusiasm for the opportunities that he was being given to share his story. He unapologetically enters a space and claims it as his own to preach his message of overcoming the obstacles of life and stepping into your destiny.

Jermaine does the work and doesn't get distracted by the naysayers and ne'er-do- wells. What Jermaine has done best is to glom onto people who want to see him do well. He takes advantage of the support that is offered to him by saying yes to the mentors and people who have excelled in their respective careers. Jermaine doesn't waste time thinking about how something fails; instead, he spends time thinking about how something will succeed.

If given the opportunity, I wouldn't change anything about the path Jermaine and I have taken to get to this day. I poked, prodded and provoked him to dot his i's and cross his t's, and to trust his intuition. When his effectiveness was evident, I asked him to think beyond the audience that he was serving and to consider different mediums for spreading his message. His confidence and inner compass have served him well. He has rejected any opinion or "critical" feedback that did not serve his purpose or direct him towards his goal of reaching people and delivering his message of hope. Such a trait has elevated him to new heights and aspirations only winners can envision.

One of the best things I've learned from him was to get out of my own way and encourage others to do the same. I know for a fact that he's unafraid to go down the path that feels right, even if it has never been trod before. So why Jermaine?

Jermaine's personal story and commitment to action and excellence separate him from the pack of the stereotypical motivational speaker. He is distinguishable as a leader and is an inspirational force for a generation that needs true, authentic role models. I look forward to his continued ascendency into the motivational speaker space so that he can fulfill his life's purpose.

Why Jermaine?

Susanne Mancheno

I've known Jermaine for over about 13 years. I knew him originally as a family man and husband, to a friend. I knew him as a man who kept a roof over their head, food on the table, and arms open with love. He has always encompassed all that is good in a man from what I have seen. Since the beginning, he was always a man determined to get somewhere. He never shared too much about where this somewhere would be. But clearly, he was a man with a vision. Everything he did, he did with full intent, determination and conviction. Eventually, as I gained his trust and friendship, he began to share his vision of all that he could do, and all that he could change in many. It has been an honor to have been on the journey with him from conception to this great place we are now. I have seen him grow, I have seen doors open, I have seen doors closed, as God intended, to keep him on his path. I have seen him share with many and expose his most vulnerable parts so others may learn from his journey. He does not ever leave a stone unturned. and does not ever leave a mission unaccomplished. If there is good to be done, and kindness to be shared, he is the man to do it. In summary, he has the drive like a locomotive, universal logic like Gandhi, and a heart like Mother Theresa. In the years I have known him, I have seen him be one of the most resourceful people I have ever met. He knows how to use the gifts placed before him, and how to share those gifts exponentially through his methods. His smile is infectious, and his

13

energy is contagious. I'm excited for all the future holds for him and those he touches. He's one of those people that I would say that by knowing him, you simply become a better person. Cheers to the man that inspires many. This is why I stay close always.

Why Jermaine?

Darlene Anderson

One of the most valuable practices of leadership that I hold near and dear to my heart is that of servitude. A great leader understands that it is a voluntary act of his supporters to trust his actions for the betterment of the collective. In that gift, the leader must understand the need of the collective and pledge to be faithful to the mission. Leaders uplift the masses and not themselves. Jermaine Jones exudes this characteristic of leadership. He has a natural desire to not only work towards reform for the underserved but to equip aspiring influencers with the resources and practices to become tomorrow's leaders.

Jermaine's works are selfless, strategic, and time sensitive. He understands the elevation of communities requires the efforts of many, yet it starts with the daily dedication of one; each day that he's given the opportunity, he serves in that capacity.

Why Jermaine?

Chad Cisneros
Communications Professional

The first time I encountered Jermaine was when he spoke at our organization's summit called the Perfect Experience in Spring 2018. Hearing him speak about his life, his journey and his perspectives on the challenges he faced was not only inspiring for myself, but also for the over 500 people listening to him present. The way he spoke, the words he used, and his focus on certain words and details were incredible. His ability to captivate an audience through just his words made myself, and everyone, want to strive to be better both in their professional and personal lives. During his presentation, he mentioned he work at Penn Station, and living in New York as well, I'd hope that one day God would cross our paths together.

On Christmas Eve 2018, I was planning to take a trip to Vermont for Christmas and while I was waiting for my train, I hear a voice that sounded so familiar and my head perked up. I looked and there I saw Jermaine helping out two people who seemed lost. I felt this innate urge to walk up and simply say hi and the impact of his speech had on me. The moment I introduced myself, Jermaine immediately treated me like a brother – shaking my hand and wanting a photograph. I never felt so much kindness and love from a person who I hardly knew, and Jermaine was so warming and excited to have met me. He was so grateful and happy that I came up to speak to him. He walked me to my train, kindly put my bag up in the rafters and we exchanged numbers to connect in the future.

It's been a true blessing to have Jermaine alongside my journey of life. He is a man who I've grown to respect even more – to understand his heart, to hear the challenges he faces and to see how he overcomes them. He's been a true role model and mentor for me – someone you can throw your thoughts and ideas at and he'd give you a genuine answer because he wants the best for you. That's a rarity these days.

I believe in what God has commissioned him to do. It's clear in what God has blessed him with – his ability to connect with people, how he is able to captivate you with his speaking talents, and he is a man on a mission. Despite any challenges or hurdles that he encounters through life or people, he is able to still push forward and accomplish the task at hand.

I think the simplest way to put it is: Continue to push forward regardless of the hurdles one may face from others or life. Anytime you do God's work, you are bound to face obstacles, but with the right mindset and continuing to trust in yourself and your belief, you will continue to push forward.

I would say the greatest takeaway I've learned from Jermaine is about the perspective you have in challenges and even achievements. A simple mental shift can make all the difference in your outlook on life. And listening to Jermain's life, every achievement came from thinking differently and more positively about the situation.

Why Jermaine?

Sherwin L. Bentick

High School: Immaculate Conception Montclair, NJ

College: Sage College of Albany, NY (Sophomore)

I first met Mr. Jones when I was in the Internship Program for the Essex County Prosecutor's Office. He was one of our guest speakers throughout the program. While I was in this program, my cousin told me, "take advantage of it and network." Many speakers came to share about their past and what they are now doing to impact society as a whole. Jermaine stood out from all the speakers gave their testimony. I went up to him and we had a conversation. He then proceeded to give me his card.

That night I looked at the business card and said to myself, "this card holds a tremendous amount of value and power," I then used it and sent him an email. Over the next couple of days, I received a response from Mr. Jones about meeting my family and I. From there, we got everything together and my mother and I began our journey to Belleville, NJ to meet Mr. Jones. When we got there, we proceeded inside, and I was looking around from Mr. Jones. At first, I couldn't recognize him because I was expecting him to be wearing a full suit and tie, but instead, he was wearing sweatpants, a long sleeve shirt, and sneakers. This showed me that no matter who you are, you're still a person and you can be yourself without having to dress in a particular manner. In today's society, we put pressure on people of a higher class, and title to have to wear a specific type of clothing in order to represent themselves, when in reality, it should not be this way. My mentorship with Mr. Jones began to grow after our first meeting because he made it clear it's not just him and myself, but that my family is a part of it as well. Also, Mr. Jones is a very humble man, who carries himself with dignity and does not let anything get in the way of his goals. The reason I decided to support Mr. Jones is because of his drive to help others, especially kids, teens, and young adults from the inner city like myself. The advice that I would give to someone that wants to take the same path Mr. Jones did is: you have to be determined, have the right mindset, set different goals, and have a reason behind your drive to do it.

Even though I've seen crazy things and been through very hectic situations in life, I would not change a thing. In Sociology, which is my minor, I learned a term similar to PTSD (Post Traumatic Stress Disorder) called PTG (Post Traumatic Growth). This means growing from any experience that you have had in life. One thing that Mr. Jones impacted was my overall outlook on life, by allowing me to understand that something might not be what you think it is, it might be helpful and beautiful on one side, but nasty and ugly on the other. "What you see is not always what you get" - Jermaine Jones; this applies to every aspect of life, and what Mr. Jones has instilled in me to this day.

Over the last two years I have known him, Mr. Jones has helped me become the young man I am today. Even though I am away at college, which is extremely far away from him, making it impossible to meet with one another regularly, he is still impacting my life. Mr. Jones goes out of his way every day, or when possible, to send me a message saying little things like "Consistency is the Key!" or "There comes a time in your life, when you cross paths of a diamond, make sure you take the time to appreciate and value that diamond, because you may never see it again in your lifetime". Lastly, Jermaine Jones is an amazing and influential man that I am grateful to have in my life.

Why Jermaine?

Ibn Wallace

Graduate, Montclair State University

Class of 2020

My friend, who is more like my brother, and I are in Montclair, NJ coming out of Panera Bread on our way to Smashburger, which happen to be across from one another. My friend is not the biggest fan of Panera, but I love it so, I decided we can go to Smashburger; as we debated in the parking lot, he referred to me as his N-word in a "friendly way." In the moment, I thought nothing of it until I heard "Brother, brother, hey my brother do you know what that word means and you're screaming it out referring it to each other as it? Come on, you are better than that!" At first, I stopped and thought "who is this guy, and does he not understand this wasn't meant to be offensive?" The word is used so loosely in popular culture, that I didn't realize how much I was being disrespected. So, when Mr. Jones pitched me Brothers Making a Difference, I thought I knew it all as I knew the magnitude of the word and how detrimental it was for people to use it. As I began to defend my friend as if I was his attorney, I thought, let me listen and gain more wisdom before I open my mouth to speak. Mr. Jones said, "listen to what you are really saying" and stopped for a moment to pause to let us think. "Are you kidding me, how old are you?" My response was honest, innocent, and naive "16, sir I'm 16." Then Mr. Jones looked to my brother and said "and yourself?" "...I just turned 17." Mr. Jones gave me a history lesson which was completely non-verbal, a simple look that changed my perspective forever.

Mr. Jones then began to introduce himself "Hello, young men, my name is Jermaine Jones and I am the founder of Brothers Making a Difference." I didn't even know what a founder was until I got home, googled it and vetted his work. There were a few articles at the time because BMAD was just getting started. I didn't understand what true mentorship was until we engaged with one another overtime.

Jermaine showed me what work ethic is; confirmation of what my father preached my entire life. Jermaine taught me how to do business with integrity. Initially, I thought to myself why would this guy be interested in helping a young brother like myself? It took for me to see the value within myself to understand, "you know I deserve to be treated with respect, carry myself with honor, and genuinely help other people all in the same light."

Prior to meeting Jermaine, I was not Mr. Ibn Wallace. My confidence was low, I accepted slander from others and didn't have the ability to say NO! The constant mentorship at Panera by Jermaine allowed me to find the man in myself that I needed to be for myself first, and of course, my family. Jermaine would catch me if I was falling by the side. Since I was a commuter student, I would come up with silly excuses like "well there's no wi-fi at my house and Panera doesn't have a VPN, so no homework will be done tonight." Then I'd have that big, loud voice in the back of my head - "I WAS FIGHTING DEPRESSION WITH NOBODY TO CALL!" From those words, I would find inner strength and know my problems aren't bigger than me. My challenges do not define me, I can do all things! My faith became stronger. I would dig much deeper into the dream that I knew I deserved – to bring my mom the degree she never had! It all comes back to wanting to quit, but Jermaine not letting me.

The BMAD no excuses policy is so real! I would find myself at Panera with a 5-page paper due, no food in the fridge at my mom's apartment and nobody to call. Who would pop up out of nowhere? Mr. Jermaine Jones. It would be heroic, and I'm not the type of person to tell stories just to beef up another person, I just wasn't raised that way. So, to his sponsors, I would like to say thank you for being able to feed me when I couldn't feed myself. I would be employed during the rough times and wouldn't be able to get my finances together, and Jermaine would give me tips and tools to get right back on track. He would simply say "never be afraid to pick up the phone and call someone and let them know your situation." I gradually built a trust in Mr. Jones, where I would sacrifice my time and energy to work on projects with him, or just soak up his energy. You don't take people like Mr. Jones for granted because there's always someone else wishing to have that personal time with a C.E.O. as I have.

I support Mr. Jones because he is someone filled with the spirit, swarming a room, feeding people like it was his job; not only feeding people but serving people with a purpose. I met him once and my life did a 180 degree turn by just one word: sacrifice. I felt privileged compared to the pain I felt in his personal story. Things were horrid at home. I had no leverage in terms of how I would support myself, get solid rest, and become successful, but Mr. Jones kept telling me "consistency is key!" I believed it and it followed me all the way to becoming the first one in my family to obtain a college degree.

In talking about support, Jermaine gave me an amazing opportunity to shine and use my talents. The day before my birthday, I just so happened to be at Panera eating lunch with Jermaine and he invited me down to Wilmington, Delaware with his team because he was the Keynote speaker for the YMCA of Wilmington Delaware, Black Achievers banquet. I had just started my media business and he told me to come take pictures "if I can." I would have to find a way to get it done and in the back of my mind I kept thinking "faith of a mustard seed!" This event was so special to me because of the amazing line-up of guest speaker; it exceeded my expectations. My career essentially started that week and I captured the footage of the Mayor of Delaware, Michael Purzycki, giving Mr. Jones the key to the city. By faith, integrity, and passion, I now have a career that I love, with the degree to accompany it, because I didn't quit.

I would advise someone who wants to follow in Jermaine's footsteps that everything is not just about money; change your perspective and learn how to give. Once you start giving more to yourself and others, you'll be able to give more and more. It's real, opportunity is cyclical, it's about who you serve. Majority of communication is non- verbal - people can genuinely see your heart. You'll never know whose life you can touch, when you genuinely want to help others. When you have $0 in your pocket, you still have something to give. If given the opportunity to do it all over again - the hunger, stress, pain, patience, joy, tears, and love, of course, I would do it with no questions; God's timing is perfect!

One thing I've learned from Jermaine that has impacted my outlook on life is to be consistent. Consistency will carry me over the top to become the C-Suite executive that I aspire to become. It's amazing what God's favor can do for your life when you are consistent and persistent in what you believe.

Why Jermaine?

Eden Fowler Benton

The first time I met Jermaine, he was a speaker for an internship with which I was involved. The program was a 6-week program, and all the speakers prior to Jermaine had been a drag. When Jermaine walked in the room, we all just had a great feeling about him, his energy spread through the room like wildfire. After he spoke, I made sure to thank him for his time and ask for a business card so I could send a follow-up thank you. Overtime, Jermaine and I kept in contact and stayed abreast on how one another were doing in life and career wise. After the first time I met Jermaine, I knew he was a great contact to keep.

Supporting Jermaine was a no brainer. Jermaine was a speaker for my internship group during the summer of 2015, and I still remember a quote from when he initially spoke. He said, "never look down on another person unless you are going to pick them up." Someone that has a mindset and story as moving as Jermaine's deserves to have a large following. If anyone wants to take a similar path as Jermaine, I would simply tell them to keep a positive mind, network as much as possible and treat others how you want to be treated.

Jermaine's story resonated with me and I raved about it for weeks following. If I had the opportunity to do it all again, I absolutely would. The one thing I learned from Jermaine that impacted my outlook on life was his life story. He told my internship group that he used to be extremely negative, but changed his entire perspective to positivity, and because of that, he prospered. Seeing how positivity changed Jermaine's whole life around made me want to do the same. Remembering all that Jermaine said to my group back in 2015 made me want to be a supporter for all things that he did moving forward.

Why Jermaine?

Dawn Monique Edmond
CEO, Enid-Books Corp.

Jermaine's infectious energy, enthusiasm, drive, and magnetic smile has catapulted him into the hearts and memory of many. When Jermaine is not extending himself to assist frustrated passengers or calm an impatient, worried crowd in his position as Station Manager at New York Penn Station, he is making random, pop-up visits at public schools mentoring the youth. I witnessed, firsthand, Jermaine's ability to capture and hold the attention of a large group of middle school boys, and that is no easy feat. What started with the "class clown," a few hecklers and a click of rowdy friends ended with the disruptors sitting quietly and intently listening to him speak.

Jermaine used his life's trials and tribulations to connect with the children, sharing with them that he wasn't always the man that stood before them, that he too was a class clown. He grew up in the same neighborhoods as them, went to the same schools, and faced the same challenges. He used the moment to teach the boys about accountability, responsibility, respect, and perseverance. In the end, hands were being raised to ask questions or make comments about the issues they were facing.

Why Jermaine? Was it his family issues he dealt with in his childhood that caused him to want to mentor young boys? Was losing his job after many years what caused him to want to motivate the everyday working person? Or, was it the day he sat in his yard, in the rain, with the fear of not being able to provide for his family overwhelming him, that caused him to want to serve the homeless? All those things combined with the many other issues and obstacles he has faced could be why he founded the nonprofit organization, Brothers Making a Difference, where he positively impacts the lives of many.

Why Jermaine? Jermaine has a way of meeting people where they are, without judgment, but with empathy, compassion, and patience. Whether it is the homeless man he is feeding, the young child in the school he mentors, the executive in corporate America, or the waitress who takes his meal order, Jermaine "treats everyone like they are the CEO." An interaction with Jermaine is unforgettable. Why not Jermaine?

Why Jermaine?

John Berry Jr.
President & CEO,
Richmond Region Tourism

I have been in the public assembly facilities and hospitality industry throughout my 40-year career. I have been in charge of facilities hosting the public including arenas, convention centers and have hosted major sporting events. The common thread has been handling crowds and dealing with the public.

In August of 2017, my family took AMTRAK to New York City for a mini-vacation and to watch a Broadway show. At the conclusion of our weekend, we were at Penn Station awaiting our train to return to Richmond, Virginia. The station was packed with people. It had to be over 500-600 people scattered throughout and no one in any line, or in any specific order. When all of a sudden, a train departing for Boston had its track announced. It seemed that the entire human mass of people was all converging on the track's entrance. At that time a gentleman wearing a necktie, with no public announcement system, and no megaphone, from the center of the station, took charge of the masses. With an authoritative tone, not overbearing, not derogatory, but with calmness, told the crowd to politely que up for that particular track number. What transpired next was a lifelong memory. The crowd obeyed his commands with precision. Once the order was established, I walked up and exclaimed how impressed I was by what I had witnessed. I was expecting just a nice acknowledgment and 11 have a nice day" but this was not the case. Jermaine Jones engaged me in conversation about Penn Station and AMTRAK, all the while, he was directing others to other tracks and other destinations. It was the most impressive display of crowd control I had ever witnessed.

We exchanged business cards, and once again, I thought that this would be the end of our brief relationship. Upon returning to Richmond, I wrote to the President of Amtrak and explained to him about our experience with Jermaine and Penn Station. The president did respond to my letter. However, I did not realize the depth of Jermaine.

We have kept in touch weekly since our first encounter. I have since learned about Jermaine's nonprofit organization, Brothers Making a Difference. I have learned about his relationship with the CEO's of Panera, and CEO's of other corporations. Also, as no surprise to me or anyone who knows Jermaine, in 2019 he was awarded the Presidential Award for AMTRAK-#1 in the country!!

I have been truly blessed to have had the pleasure of meeting Jermaine several years ago. He has had a tremendous effect on many lives including mine.

Why Jermaine?

Zelia "Zee" Oliveira

Director, Boy & Girls Club
Newark Ironbound

When I first met Mr. Jermaine, there was no doubt in my mind that we were meant to come across each other's paths. I always knew that there were good people in this world, but Mr. Jermaine is GREAT! He has the biggest heart anyone can have. Mr. Jermaine came into our club as a guest speaker and immediately captured the attention of our kids. All ears opened from ages 6-56; he shared his story with us and captivated our hearts into helping him, help others! Our teens quickly agreed that his mission is one they wanted to be part of, and they were! Today, when they hear the name Mr. Jermaine, they connect it with kindness and hope. I am honored to have had the pleasure of meeting Mr. Jermaine Jones.

The feelings I have when I see Mr. Jones are of HOPE! He does not judge anyone, instead he looks for ways to help people become better. There is no decision making once you meet Mr. Jones, you automatically " jump on his train." You know that he is always up to doing something GOOD! Advice I would give someone who wants to follow a similar path to Jermaine's is always stay on track, as he constantly repeats, "consistency is KEY," and that is the truth. Without a doubt, 1 will always want to be a part of Mr. Jermaine's journey. HE MAKES A DIFFERENCEI!!!

One thing I've learned is when a door closes, a window of opportunity awaits you!!! He never gave up on HIMSELF and he never gives up on others!

These are qualities one cannot learn; this is called
PASSION! I will always believe in him and his
DREAM!

Why Jermaine?

Aleia K. Brown, MPA
CEO, Moore2LifeMotivations, LLC

I met Jermaine about 8 years ago, while I was a Director at a non-profit looking for males to mentor the youth we served. What I immediately noticed about Jermaine was his contagious and boisterous laugh - you can't help but be in a good mood in his presence. During that meeting, we discussed mentorship for youth, and our vision and goals for the future. I had mentioned to him that I had started a speaking business and he shared with me that he was going to start a nonprofit, and asked would I be interested in joining his team – of course, I said yes! After our first meeting, I remember saying to Jermaine "I think this is the beginning of a great partnership that will last even beyond my time in this position," and that is true to this day.

I remember the first, of many, times I volunteered to help feed the hungry with Jermaine, he had so much excitement to be of service to those in need, never demeaning anyone and making everyone, from the homeless people getting food, to the volunteers lined up to serve, feel like one big happy family. Later, Jermaine, remembering our early conversations, would offer me opportunities to speak at some of the schools he's visited, recommended as a guest speaker for a conference, shared useful information or just a kind message to keep moving forward. Even after I had to step away as my family expanded, Jermaine would always call or text to check on us. I can always look forward to an inspirational text at the most appropriate time and I'm so grateful for his friendship.

When Jermaine called me and told me he was embarking on creating his first book and what the concept was, I was ecstatic! Now everyone else would get a glimpse into what so many of us had experienced in meeting Jermaine. I was even more honored that he not only shared his plan with me, but that he asked me to be part of this project. Now, Jermaine and I laugh as he jokes that every time he sees my husband, who also works on the rails, he thanks him and tells him he'll have his wife back soon, since we've been working together.

One of the many great lessons that I've learned from Jermaine is: to be successful, you have to out think, out plan and out work everyone else and be willing to do what others won't – go the extra mile! Jermaine is a doer of good works and doesn't just give lip service. His journey thus far is a testament to his dedication and ability to "be the hardest worker in the room."

Why Jermaine?

Brenda Green
CEO, Fit 4 A Better Me, LLC

I first met Jermaine at a Brothers Making a Difference feed the homeless event that took place under a bridge near Penn Station in Newark, NJ in Feb 2017. It came at a perfect time when I was trying to teach my 5-year-old daughter about giving. I arrived right on time as the staff was setting up on this cold chilling night. I was immediately welcomed by Jermaine's big bright smile and a firm handshake. I was truly impressed; I initially thought it might be some sandwiches, snacks with water but when the food arrived from a local restaurant, pans of rice and chicken were on the menu that night. My daughter and I immediately went to work. Hat and gloves on, I placed rice on everyone's plate while my daughter handed out bottles of water with a smile of excitement. As I looked down the table to check on her, I knew a seed was planted.

How can we continue doing this, I thought? We were both so excited to be there. As I was working, I had the pleasure to get a glimpse of Jermaine. It was inspiring watching him interact with everyone. It didn't matter who you were, he greeted the police officer the same way he greeted each homeless person who passed by with the same big bright smile and a handshake. At that moment, I realize this man is the real deal. Days after, I was still in a state of gratitude. Having the opportunity to give back and share that moment with my daughter was truly priceless.

My daughter and I attended a few more events that year. Around Christmas time, I reached out to Jermaine because I was looking for charity work to do with my daughter. Unfortunately, he wasn't doing anything, but a seed had already been planted. The moment my cousin called me because he was looking for charity work to do with his kids that's when the seed sprouted and became the Kids Blessing Bag Project.

The goal is to have the kids involved from beginning to end in the giving back process. The kids have to earn their money by doing chores, physically go to the store with the money they earned and purchase the items assigned. Everyone's purchases were combined, and the kids put the bags together. Once the bags were assembled the parents and kids drove and parked under the same bridge near Penn Station in Newark and walked around the area handing out the bags.

In 2017, we were able to put together 20 bags and 15 kids participated. The impact the project had on the kids and the parents was incredible. The following year, we doubled the number of kids and the bags given, 50 bags with approximately 35 kids. Cash donations came in as well, and Jermaine donated the biggest amount that year. His donation allowed me to create 12 more bags. Again, proving he is a man of his word.

This project came into fruition all because Jermaine followed his calling. For that, I am truly thankful as we are entering the third year of the Kids Blessing Bag Project. Jermaine taught me that giving back doesn't have to be complicated, it can be as simple as a big smile and a firm handshake to let the person know you are there.

Why Jermaine?

Robert Davis

For the life of me, I can't remember when, where or how I initially met Jermaine. We both, to this day, ask ourselves that question. It's so ironic. However, I do remember when we first had an opportunity to work together, and for me, that seems like the first experience I've had with Jermaine that I can remember.

It was nighttime, in the fall, in downtown Newark outside of Penn Station. My sister and I had decided that we would go downtown and meet with Jermaine to help him feed the less fortunate. All I can remember is seeing him in his white car parked in the back of Penn Station with a trunk full of food from Cuban Pete's restaurant. He was standing there pulling food from the trunk and placing it on the ledge of a building. I was so perplexed!!! I remember looking at my sister, and my sister looking back at me, and we both had the same exact look on our face, "like this guy has absolutely no clue what the hell he is doing!!" We both whispered to each other "is he really going to let homeless people serve themselves?" We so desperately wanted to interject and say "hey Jermaine, you know there's a better way to do this?," but we hadn't had any previous experience with him, or his organization, so we didn't want it to seem as if we were taking over his initiative. While we were attempting to set up, I believe I stepped out on faith and said "hey man, you know we should try doing this differently, especially when it comes down to serving people on the street"

To my surprise, Jermaine welcomed ALL suggestions with open arms. He said something to the effect, "hey, if you have a better way of doing this, by all means, go right ahead. I have no problem with letting someone else take the lead." At that point, I knew things between us were going to be alright.

Over time, I gained a true sense of gratitude and appreciation. I felt blessed to have the opportunity to work with, support, encourage, laugh with, pray with and cry with a man who continues to live a service-based, selfless life. I would absolutely say appreciation is the word that comes to mind when I thing of Jermaine, I appreciate the fact that he is intentional about mostly everything in his life, but most importantly, his willingness just to check up on his friends and share a positive word on a daily basis.

It's quite easy to support an individual who has like-minded interests. Jermaine and I are quite similar when it comes down to the calling that has been placed on our lives. The bible says "obedience is better than sacrifice," so with that, the God in me recognizes the God in him, and it makes nothing but total sense to serve and support in any capacity, the things that God, obviously, has placed upon his heart and head. A true leader is never intimidated by another individual's greatness. They are actually attracted to that greatness and want to grow in areas where they may have perceived deficiencies. We are all her to grow and learn from each other!

Advice for someone wanting to follow a similar path as Jermaine – DON'T!!!!! LOL If you've ever spent any significant amount of time with Jermaine, you will come to find out, quickly, that you do not have enough energy to keep up with or sustain the pace in which he operates. I like to believe that life is a marathon, not a sprint. That mindset clearly does not resonate with Jermaine. Jermaine is essentially sprinting his marathon!!! LOL Moral of the story is – if you'd like to follow a path similar to Jermaine's, you must be EXTREMELY intentional about every aspect of your day, life, time and purpose! We haven't stopped yet, but I would ABSOLUTELY, WITHOUT HESITATION, do it all over again.

Jermaine is a walking soundbite! If you've been around him for any significant amount of time, you've heard the following:

- Consistency is the key.

-I may not be the sharpest tool in the shed, but I can still make the cut.

- Never look down on a man unless you are there to pick him up.

- Save one life at a time.

The single most influential aspect of interacting with Jermaine over the years would be the understanding that your previous setbacks and short comings does not have to be the end of your story. Every day, you can go out and change your situation and circumstance, if you want. If you believe in something hard enough, have discipline and remain persistent and positive, you can overcome any obstacle that life throws you.

Why Jermaine?

Sgt. Manuel Cancel II

I first met Jermaine some time ago, when he started coming in as a sub for one of our bowlers. He was probably the happiest person I had ever met. It seemed like his life was perfect. I had gotten to know more about him as he came around more often. He was working for DHL at the time, and he advised me that he was involved in a mentorship program. He would take a few underprivileged boys around to different places and give them a chance to experience life outside of their neighborhood. He didn't just stop there, he made sure that everyone he mentored learned what it meant to be a man, what it meant to have responsibilities and that each one of us is accountable for our actions. What he did was prepare a lot of these young boys to learn to become men. Many of these young men come from single parent homes, where dad is no longer in the picture, for whatever reason.

During this whole time, I sat in amazement listening to the stories he would tell about one of his boys and how he was able to turn his life for the better. Now, that young man is going to be a future mentor. That's when I learned about Jermaine's plan to begin a mentorship program for boys and girls. This concept is what has now become known as "Brothers Making a Difference"

Let me digress a moment. This didn't just happen overnight for Jermaine. He went through some trials and was tested several times. The average man would not have survived, but Jermaine is not the average man. This man remained focused and continues to be an inspiration for all. I am currently a Sergeant in the police department of one of the largest metropolitan areas in NJ, and it goes without saying that I have seen people at their worst, as well as at their best. Anytime I'm feeling down about the world and what we leave behind for our children, I remind myself that there is still some good in the world and all we have to do is look for it. Jermaine is living proof of that and the good that can come out of it, if we just give it a chance to grow. I have had the privilege to call him a friend, but I have the pleasure to call him my brother.

Why Jermaine?

David Herndon

When I first met Jermaine, he was new to Amtrak. He was energetic. He had a spark - a type of energy that I had never seen in a person. He always has an exuberant amount of energy! You just don't expect that kind of enthusiasm. Most people with that kind of enthusiasm make you wonder. I remember thinking, "What's his angle? Is this dude for real or is this all an act?" As I got to know him, I was like, "Wow! That's really who he is." Jermaine is authentic. His faith is extraordinarily strong. He has told me about his struggles and how he has overcome major challenges in his life. Through his trials, he has learned to celebrate life and share his joy.

Since he has been at Amtrak, he is a consistently good brother. He is a natural, people person. He talks to any and EVERYBODY! He just has so much energy and excitement; his personality is infectious. It's hard to be around him and feel bad about life. When I was going through my own personal challenges, this brother was always there encouraging me. "It's gonna be okay. You have to believe that and hang in there". He was one of a handful of people that was there for me. He is original and unique. Most people don't have charisma of that magnitude. I'm proud to see such a hard-working, life-loving man move up through the company.

When Jermaine started his own company, Brothers Making a Difference, with $19 in his checking account, his faith endured; he knew he would find a way. I also knew that whatever he touched was going to be successful. His passion for humanity is a catalyst for change. He inspires others to pay attention to the human condition.

Whether he is feeding the homeless or taking students to a New York Jets football game, he touches lives. He is a change agent that shares powerful information and provides impactful moments and supports.

People have witnessed his strengths and are mesmerized by his leadership qualities. As a result, Jermaine now travels around the country speaking at various companies to motivate teams to be their best. Jermaine remains humble and appreciative. If you are around him, you will hear him say, "Always put God first!" Every time I see Jermaine, he offers words of encouragement. He is an inspiration to many. I'm proud to know such an amazing brother. I wish him well with his book venture.

Why Jermaine?

Larry Drexler

General Counsel & Chief Privacy Officer
Barclays Bank Delaware

Some may say Jermaine Jones is lucky. I disagree. A high school coach once described luck as preparation meeting opportunity. Jermaine spent a lifetime preparing and when the opportunity train came, Jermaine jumped on to ride with the engineer.

Jermaine was endowed from birth with a sharp mind, no doubt inherited from his mother, as she is sure to tell you - quick wit, an innate sense of people, a keen sense of observation, a drive to succeed and a willingness to work hard. There is no doubt that Jermaine had the potential to be successful in any endeavor, but, for a period of time, that potential went untapped. In retrospect, he spent the first part of his life in survival mode, not mining his gifts for anything other than providing for his family. And how could you blame him? He grew up surrounded by addiction and poverty. His focus was to provide for his family. His drive was not just providing for his family, but also making sure that they would have a better opportunity. Even then, the seeds of what is to come were sown.

Jermaine worked for a freight transport company. For the most part, his gifts were unrealized. Then his world was turned upside down when he lost his job after a corporate restructuring. While the days immediately following were dark, the aftermath set the stage for his gifts to be nurtured and exploited. From that despair, came a new world view. Jermaine awoke to the realization that providing for his family was not enough, he needed to provide for his community. He vowed that once he was back on his feet, he would not forget his community. He learned it was better to lead than to follow, and leadership came easy to him. Just ask the folks at the Newark Employment office!

In Jermaine's case, the light at the end of the tunnel was actually a train, an Amtrak train. Amtrak gave Jermaine a stage. Not only did he work hard every day, he got to perform. Jermaine started as a baggage handler, the lowest rung on the ladder.

Jermaine committed to being the best baggage handler, not just at Penn station, but ever. In doing so, his sense of observation kicked in. He was able to see the behaviors in others that inhibited their success. Jermaine did not just observe, he made it his mission to not let those behaviors stop him, and now others.

As a baggage handler, Jermaine's interactions were one on one, but then Amtrak handed him a microphone, literally. He became a conductor. Passengers up and down the northeast corridor were treated to a personalized set of station announcements. He made it his mission to make sure every passenger had a great experience. He became a problem solver, not just his problems, or problems on the trains, but the problems passengers brought on board. Amtrak then gave Jermaine an even bigger stage, Station Master. As Station Master, his audience became thousands of people a day. To be successful, he needed to harness each of his gifts to motivate his team and manage the chaos of Penn Station. He was challenged to lead in an environment where he controls none of the elements that influenced his day. He could not control if the trains were on time, the weather, the crowds from events at MSG or the mood of the passengers. Despite these challenges, Jermaine's booming voice rises above the turmoil. With humor and understanding of the human condition, Jermaine and team safely and efficiently deliver passengers to their trains.

Success at Amtrak did not deter Jermaine from his work in the community. He started Brothers Making a Difference, a non-profit with the dual mission of feeding the homeless along with a youth outreach program to help children rise above their circumstances. Jermaine soon had another audience to lead, kids of all ages and circumstances. He began to share his story mixing humor, pathos and inspiration to motivate the children.

The opportunity came in the form of a downtrodden traveler, a very successful restaurateur from Boston, who was carrying a leadership book. He had just attended a set of meetings with students talking about leadership that he had found quite depressing. Jermaine struck up a conversation with the restauranteur. Somehow, the restauranteur took a leap of faith and invited Jermaine to share his story with the restauranteur's staff. It was, of course, an unqualified success.

A few months later, this downtrodden traveler got stuck in Penn Station: train delayed. I saw Jermaine responding to a stressed commuter and made a smart aleck comment about leadership. Jermaine responded: Leadership is learned on the floor of the station, not in a textbook. After two hours of conversation about leadership, life and which train would get me home quicker, Jermaine put me on my train. The following day, I attended a business meeting that included the topic of finding a speaker we could bring in to talk to our senior leaders about adversity and leading through change. I called the restauranteur who assured me that I was about to make the smartest decision of my life. I bit. We made the arrangements. Of course, there would be a stipend for Jermaine, but he insisted that the stipend be split with a substantial portion being a donation to Brothers Making a Difference.

A month later, Jermaine spoke to our team. He got the "coveted" spot - the second morning of the two-day event, with a bedraggled, slightly hungover audience. Jermaine delivered his inspiring and uplifting message of conquering his demons and rising above his circumstances with the force of a freight train and the comedic timing of Chris Rock. He owned the stage and the audience. The result, a standing ovation and line of senior execs asking for a picture with Jermaine. The only people disappointed were the folks who presented after Jermaine.

Some may say it was luck, I say his success is the residue of everything in his life that came before. Jermaine was well prepared for the opportunity that would find him in the Great Room at Penn Station. Two traits separate Jermaine from the pack, first he has the courage to seize the opportunity when presented, and second, he does not fear failure, not even considering failure an option. Most of us, shy away from opportunity afraid to take the risk, Jermaine leans in and conducts.

You ask: "Why Jermaine?" I ask: "Why not Jermaine?"

Why Jermaine?

Shareef Cleveland
CEO, NMS Records

My initial encounter with Jermaine was riding on the light rail train from Newark, New Jersey to Bloomfield, New Jersey. It's my daily commute home from work, and I was in uniform, standing with my back to the crowded train. With not much conversation going on inside the train, I heard a voice standing to the side of me say "How are you my brother?" I glanced for a short moment, said hello, and returned my eyes front, hoping the stranger speaking to me wasn't going to be any trouble. It is not common for anyone to speak on trains, so being in my military uniform and having someone approach me, was a red flag. It got quiet for a moment and I noticed that whomever just spoke to me was still standing there with a big smile on his face. My initial thought was 1. He might be crazy 2. He is interested in the military or 3. He might be crazy.

Our initial conversation on the train went from awkward to awarding. Jermaine's second question after asking me how I was doing, was if I ever considered working with kids. That question immediately lowered my invisible wall from conversing with a stranger to this must have been meant to be. I told Jermaine that is something I've been wanting to do for a long time, and to please inform me when there's an opportunity to volunteer.

I decided to work with Jermaine because he was well prepared in answering my questions - What is your mission, where do you volunteer and what's the goal? Consistency, dedication and leadership will put someone in the right path to do something similar to Jermaine. Given the opportunity, I would do it all over again, without hesitation.

Some things I've learned from Jermaine are: 1. Your circumstances do not determine your outcome. 2. Never look down on a man/woman unless you are going to help them up. 3. You have to learn how to follow before you can lead.

Why Jermaine?

Dan Hogan

Senior Advisor

My first introduction to Jermaine was surely unique. In fact, so much so, that I wanted to write the CEO of Amtrak to sing Jermaine's praises. Since I couldn't find an email address, I posted the following on Amtrak's Facebook page:

I wanted to write Joe Boardman, CEO of Amtrak, a note about the incredible customer service I received from Jermaine Jones, Station Manager of Penn Station in NYC. But I haven't been able to get his email address, so I've decided to post something here and hope it gets to him.

There were several parts to that service. The first was my asking Jermaine how I might find the monitors on the floor below the main floor where I could get information on track assignments ahead of the crowds on the main floor – a tip my daughter had imparted to me. He explained that this was against the rules and not allowed. He did so in a most gracious, friendly, and yet firm way. We sparred back and forth in very friendly fashion, and he convinced me this was not a good idea, in part because Amtrak needs to check everyone's ticket.

I thought that would be the end of it, but then he said that he would take care of my problem. He proceeded to locate Eric Johnston, a red cap, who took us to the Acela lounge, where we were able to relax until the train arrived. Then Eric helped us get on board in a timely fashion so that we got a seat on an oversold train (everyone was leaving for Boston early due to one of the major snowstorms we got this winter). Jermaine is an incredible asset to Amtrak, and I hope his worth is recognized.

I don't know if Joe Boardman ever saw my Facebook post, but even this year, others who have received the same sort of amazing service have added to my post. Over the next few years, I always seemed to run into Jermaine whenever I came to New York on Amtrak. He would be herding passengers to their appointed destinations, bellowing insanely funny comments to all around him and creating a wonderful atmosphere that brought out the best in all of us. Jermaine actually remembered my name, which I found hard to believe, given the number of people with whom he deals on a regular basis. I had told my children and partner all about Jermaine, because there are truly few people like him in the universe. And speaking of the universe, here's a serendipitous chance meeting that is hard to believe. It's best told by simply copying the email I received two summers ago from my older daughter, when she was at Penn Station: Guess who I met?????!! It's the stationmaster Jermaine!!!!! He was talking to these guys near me who were worried cause our train kept getting delayed and I was like smiling at him cause he was so rad and then he told the guys he was going to give them the inside track and take them to the gate so they could be first, and then he saw me and he was like you've got good energy too so follow me! And we got to the gate and I was like omg I bet this guy is Jermaine, so I say hey, what's your name and he says Jermaine, and I was like omg my dad knows you! And he says who's your dad & I say Dan Hogan and he goes crazy! He tells me well you come to the very front of the line! Your dad is an amazing man! Etc. Then he's like, "you gotta snap a pic" - he won't believe it.

Since then, we've continued to see Jermaine whenever we get to New York. And this past Thanksgiving weekend, we received a call from him saying that he was in Boston and would love to get together. It was so nice to see him outside of his work environment. Of course, Jermaine remained true to himself and we had a most delightful lunch at the Eastern Standard in Kenmore Square. It was a treat to drive him to the train station – a bit of a role reversal!!! Luckily, he made his train on time!!!

Why Jermaine?

Jason Falchuk

Founder, BioBridges

I remember the first day I met Jermaine. Our mutual friend had arranged a special dinner for some friends from a variety of businesses to get together and spend some time with Jermaine who was in town for a corporation session. My wife and I were waiting for our host to arrive and noticed a gentleman (also in the waiting area) with this smile that was larger than life. I remember whispering in my wife's ear, "that had to be him." Just as I walked over to say hello, our host arrived and made the intros. As I expected that man was Jermaine. Within minutes, he made us all feel at ease and we lost ourselves in the kind of conversations you would share with dear friends and family you haven't seen in years. It was natural and easy. I wasted no time in asking him to come into my office the next day to speak to our company. He had a packed day but said, "if it is important to you, let's make it happen." I remember how excited I was to text my team later that night and let them know I had a big surprise for all of us in the morning.

The next morning, I picked him up bright and early (7:45 am) to drive to my office. I parked and went into the hotel to greet him, and on my way up the stairs to the lobby, I heard his voice in his special way making each person feel special as he's asking, "how is your day going so far?" He was not going through motions of just asking to ask, he would wait for the response and offer something in return. I didn't want him to notice me, or interrupt him, just embrace this experience. I started to think he was doing this more so for himself than others. It was like his filter to purify the air he chose to breath. On our way to the office we stopped at Panera, familiar ground to Jermaine, who had been their keynote speaker at their big annual event at the Grand Ole Opry.

It was a story I have now heard him share over and over again, yet I never get tired. Panera had a customer who wanted their usual, which they did not have. The person who was serving the customer responded with the bad news and didn't offer a solution. Within seconds, I witnessed Jermaine jump into action. He went over to the server and the customer, introduced himself as if we were one of the hidden camera shows, exposed the situation and trained the staff on how, in the future, to respond in a positive manner. It was something like "I am so sorry we don't have that today, but we do have "xyz" which I think you would really enjoy as well. Would you like me to get one for you to try?" He asked the customer how they felt in both experiences. Everyone gathered around as he worked his magic. I remember handing him a pen to sign autographs...

I could go on and on about that first day we spent together, from the session with my company, to my one on one time together - it was inspiring and fulling. However, what I remember most is that even with a packed day, he made time to meet and spend time with my son, who like all 15-year olds in high-school, had a lot on his mind. Even in 90 degrees, dress shirt and pants on, Jermaine jumped out of my car to shoot hoops with my son so he could build trust with him. All three of us went to lunch from there, and my son and Jermaine continued wonderful discussions. My feelings about Jermaine are that whatever I thought about him, he continues to validate. That the hard work for him doesn't end. That each day is filled with opportunity and that we should always put out what we want to receive. Doing right is the only way to really live a fulfilling life.

Why Jermaine?

Michael Currington

From the first day I met Jermaine, he was a beacon of positive energy. He was hired at Amtrak as a baggage handler and I was his manager. Right away you could tell Jermaine loved helping and interacting with people. Jermaine would always be the first employee on the platforms, and in the waiting rooms, greeting the passengers with a big smile and making sure they had all the information they needed to board their train. Jermaine was truly an asset to our operation in Newark Penn Station and it showed by the large number of letters Amtrak received from passengers commending Jermaine on his customer service skills. Jermaine's work ethic and customer service skills paved the way for his accelerated growth at Amtrak. He quickly went from baggage handler to baggage foreman, and not too long after, he was promoted to Station Manager.

During his years in Newark, I had the opportunity to know Jermaine on a more personal level. Jermaine and I would sit and talk about life and our paths to Amtrak. It was during these conversations that Jermaine and I really bonded. Our relationship grew from friends to brothers, and I am blessed to have a brother like Jermaine. He is a very inspirational person who is not afraid of being himself. I remember when he started Brother's Making A Difference; he was very excited to create a platform where he could share his life story with urban area kids. His goal was, and still is, to inspire and encourage them to never give up no matter how hard life gets. Jermaine always says that his goal is to reach just one person! It turns out that over the years, Jermaine has reached many people, young and old. Jermaine is truly one of the best humans I know. He's very consistent and never deviates from being the honest, giving, caring and loyal person I've known over the years - my brother!

Why Jermaine?

Annie Jimenez

I first met Jermaine Jones on an interview with the company we both currently work for in New York City. He walked in appropriately dressed and I remember one thing - his shoes were extremely clean. To this day, his shoes are still sparkling, and you can see your reflection in them.

Mr. Jones has an amazing personality to say the least. He impressed my colleague and I; we were astonished and mesmerized by this man. At times it felt like we were being interviewed by him. He had applied more than 20 times and was thrilled that we were giving him a chance. The interview went past the normal allotted time, we normally give each applicant. We even argued who needed him more in their area, and I happened to have lost. We did hire Mr. Jones on that day.

Jermaine did very well and proceeded to move on with his career. Sometimes, people come in and out of your life for many reasons. It ended up that he became a Manager and I trained him in my department. At one point in my life, I stepped down and Jermaine happened to be my manager. Our joke to people is that I hired him nine years ago. He always says, "Do you believe it". I in turn respond, "sometimes you have an off day" and we all laugh. I will say that Jermaine is a very fair and consistent manager and always bases his decisions in that manner.

As time went on, and we got to know each other, I was impressed with all the volunteer work he was doing through his organization, Brothers Making a Difference. He organized with a friend of his who owns a restaurant to donate food to feed the homeless.

Jermaine even speaks at schools and has children of all ages write him letters. Many of those letters are hanging on his wall in his office to share with others. It is very impressive!

Jermaine also made connections with an NFL team, and has children and their parents attend the games. I happen to have had the opportunity to go to a game. I brought my Godson who was thrilled to death for the chance to come and see his favorite team play. I want to thank him for making me the coolest Godmother ever!

All kidding aside, Jermaine Jones is an amazing person and I'm glad on that day, 9 years ago, we decided to hire him. Our relationship continues to grow and we both have learned things from each other. It was hard for me to put this all down in writing. Thanks for making me a better person Jermaine, and I hope I have done the same for you.

Why Jermaine?

Drew Grisham

Director, Children & Family Services
The Salvation Army Newark

Why? Why is one of the simplest and most complex questions one can ask. At the heart of humanity, we all want to know why. Why Jermaine, in the simplest context – consistency; why Jermaine, for a more complex answer read on.

I had what I learned to be an absolute privilege of meeting Jermaine in the summer of 2015. I met Jermaine in the midst of running an eight-week summer day camp program for 60 youth in the heart of poverty stricken Newark, NJ. I felt lost, alone, and afraid that my true talents were being wasted. You see, I didn't study to work with youth. I didn't spend thousands of dollars to earn a Business degree to work with youth and families. I never pictured myself working to motivate others, to drag them along to simply "do their job". The fairy tale of college and life planning led me to believe that I would be "in the big office" directing, leading, and strategizing – making money and gaining new customers. The reality was that I was a transplant from the Midwest working with and leading people that had been affected by challenges that were unheard of to me. Drugs, violence and gangs - it's one thing to read or hear about these things on the news; it is a totally different reality to witness these battles play out on your doorstep. I had to greet young people and their families as they made their way through the dangerous streets to my facility. I was beating my head against the same wall for half a decade, hoping for change and seeing no results. Wishing for a consistent helping hand, and being letdown at every turn, takes a toll on a person.

When I met Jermaine, I was at one of the lowest points of my life. I was ready to give up, throw in the towel, hit the reset button...even contemplating if life was worth living. Unbeknownst to Jermaine or myself, our paths crossed at precisely the right time.

The day I met Jermaine started as any other day, I woke up and drowned myself in coffee; anticipated the poor attitudes and mind-numbing challenges that I'd be met with for the day. "We have a guest speaker coming, he has his own non-profit and will be a great inspiration for the kids", they tell me. "Great, more mouth service and empty promises", I thought to myself. Looking back, regretfully, my first encounter with Jermaine was the most awkward and unenthused greeting anyone could be met with. Jermaine entered the run down, overcrowded building with energy, excitement, and passion. "Good Morning" he shouted and flashed a big smile to everyone he passed, being met with a "good morning" and half eye roll as the staff pointed him to my office. "Good Morning, I'm Jermaine Jones. I'm here for the career day for the kids; and this is my mother Ms. Jones" Jermaine exclaimed with way too much energy. I responded with "Great, have a seat in the conference room and I'll grab you when we're ready." Jermaine, unphased by the lack of enthusiasm he was met with, sat in the conference room preparing his heart to speak to our young people. What happened next completely blew me away and set the tone to change my entire outlook on life.

Jermaine proceeded to talk with our young people about his life experience, he was vulnerable about the trauma he faced growing up in Irvington, NJ. He openly shared about the challenges he faced throughout his life – a high school dropout with every reason to turn to the streets and take the life to fast money and danger that so many of our young people in the urban community choose. Every eye in the room was focused on Jermaine, not one child or adult leader withholding their attention. Jermaine opened up about fighting depression, reshaping himself when he thought he had met his upper limit personally and professionally. This is where his message started to hit home.

Jermaine found himself at the end of the road with a job that he thought he would have for life, when he was laid off, along with hundreds of others. Jermaine took this setback as an opportunity for his comeback. Wow! Talk about a message that I needed to hear. Jermaine promised our young people that he would be there for them and urged them to reach out for help and guidance when needed. Skeptical of how our relationship would go on from there, I was at least inspired by his message.

Many guest speakers have come and delivered valuable information, promising to support and telling me to let them know when they were needed – only to fall off the face of the earth after they left.

This was not Jermaine, not by a long shot. A few short hours after speaking with our young people Jermaine called me to ask how he could support a back to school supply drive for our group. I was blown away. Over the next few weeks and months our relationship grew, working side by side helping the forgotten people in the community the best way we knew how. It was in this time that I gained immense respect for Jermaine's positive attitude and consistent approach to life. There was no challenge that could not be met, no question that did not have an answer. I've had the privilege to work closely with Jermaine on his journey of changing the world one life at a time. I have witnessed the impact he's made in countless lives, with mine being one of them. To see Jermaine be vulnerable and genuine with people, witness him treat a homeless person as if they were the CEO allowed me to reconnect with myself. After witnessing this firsthand I made a promise to Jermaine that I would support him in any way possible. I am happy and honored to say that our relationship has grown to a brotherhood and I continue to support him to this day.

In the years of working alongside and knowing Jermaine, I have gained many pieces of advice that I implement in my daily life and share with others along their journey. The advice I can give to someone who is feeling lost, someone who is looking to make a change but doesn't know where to start, someone who is looking for their true calling in life, it would be this: Start. You cannot get anywhere in life until you start. Take your dream and make it a reality by being true to yourself, respecting others – no matter their position in life, and being consistent. These are the values that Jermaine has helped instill in me; these are the values that have brought Jermaine along a journey that even he could not imagine. I've had the honor of seeing Jermaine speak to corporate leaders, non-profit teams, and hundreds of wide-eyed young people trying to find their way. In each setting, Jermaine has held true to his core values and presented himself in an open, vulnerable way that hits home with even the most hardened cynics. This world can beat you up, tear you down, but you...you have the power to make a change. That change starts within.

Looking back, I would not change a thing. I would still greet Jermaine in the same unenthused and skeptical way. I would be weary of his promise to support and cautious in trusting him. It was my vulnerability that allowed Jermaine to see the true me and be a constant support in spite of it all. Jermaine's consistency truly changed my outlook on life, and for that, I am forever grateful.

Why Jermaine?

Det. C. Brooks

My name is Detective C. Brooks and I had the pleasure of meeting Mr. Jermaine Jones 7 years ago at Branch Brook Park in Newark NJ. I was working a special detail that day for an event with the former Mayor. Jermaine and I connected very well from the start. I was given a t-shirt and was formally introduced to "BMAD" - Brothers Making A Difference. That was my beginning of an amazing journey with Jermaine Jones.

Jermaine Jones is an amazing person. He's committed, sincere, and very dedicated to his vision as well as others. Jermaine's honesty, determination to make change when others may give up, his skills and motivation to inspire others, and overall, his dedication to never turn his back on anyone, nor look down on others are all the reasons why I decided to support Jermaine.

I would advise someone who wants to follow a similar path to be willing to sacrifice everything. They should be prepared for the setbacks, rejection, betrayal, the blood and sweat, and the sleepless days and nights." One should be willing to put in the work, even the times when all will fail you, and you're left alone.

This spectacular journey has taught me balance and character; to be STRONG, HONEST, and DETERMINED. Most importantly, it taught me to TRUST In GOD for everything, big or small, and to NEVER GIVE UP!

A quote from Jermaine Jones that I will NEVER forget: "NEVER LOOK DOWN ON A MAN, UNLESS YOU'RE GOING TO PICK HIM UP." Mr. Jermaine Jones is truly a BROTHER THAT'S MAKING A DIFFERENCE - ONE LIFE AT A TIME! You're truly loved my good brother... GOD BLESS!

Why Jermaine?

Robert Lorenzo

Engineering Instructor

After briefly meeting Jermaine at an IHOP, I had the pleasure to meet him again when he came to our school to give a motivational speech to our robotics team. I was immediately impressed with Mr. Jones' energy. He greeted every adult and every student he passed in the hall as if they were the CEO of a Fortune 500 company. Mr. Jones' energy is infectious, and his upbeat demeanor immediately hooked the students. When he began to speak, he shared words and a personal story with which the students, and myself, immediately connected. He left you on the edge of your seat waiting to hear what would come next. He made you feel you could do anything and accomplish any goal by simply changing your mindset. I have been left with a deep respect for Mr. Jones and appreciate his continued mentorship through text message.

As mentioned, Mr. Jones has a unique personality. As you get to know him, he is magnetic, humble, and models what excellence looks like. He empowers you to reach deep down to find the leader in yourself. He challenges you in a way where you never doubt your own ability to be the best you. He constantly reminds you that the road less traveled isn't easy, but there won't be much traffic in your lane either. My respect for him has and continues to grow.

Most recently Mr. Jones sent a message showing what taking the road less traveled looks like: a workout at the gym at 4 in the morning, and the gym was empty. That was such a simple message, yet something deep inside my brain heard it. For the past week or so, I have been getting up much earlier than my usual time. Jermaine has this effect, where what he says is so real and easy to connect with that when he says something you believe it and know it to be true. He sets a high bar, and without having to push, motivates you to want to always be improving yourself. Further, I am grateful to Mr. Jones for giving me another chance. It was my responsibility to reach out to him to schedule a meeting, and I failed. Shortly after the time he anticipated to hear from me, he contacted me. His doing so modeled what leadership looks like, and again, it is my pleasure to support Mr. Jones.

Advice for someone wanting to follow a similar path - recharge your batteries frequently and often. Figure out who you, are and your why, in order to ignite a similar passion to that which Mr. Jones displays. It has been an honor and a privilege getting to know Mr. Jones. My outlook on my own leadership abilities has increased tremendously. Meeting Mr. Jones has empowered me to be a better teacher and mentor for my students, and I am humbled and thankful for his support. I would not change a thing.

Mr. Jones has shared many motivating, inspiring, and uplifting stories with me over the year or so we have known each other. However, one of the most meaningful was the story I previously shared. Knowing Jermaine as well as I have been able to, his words, actions, and messages have a lot of meaning.

His recent text really inspired me to wake up earlier and seize the day. Going the extra mile may use a little more gas, but the road won't be crowded, and the road ahead is yours.

Thank you, Mr. Jones, for allowing me to participate. It has been a pleasure reflecting on our relationship.

Why Jermaine?

Garrett Harker
Owner, Eastern Standard
Restaurant

My first meeting with Jermaine was an example of how the most ordinary day can turn extraordinary if you open yourself up, even a little bit. I heard him before I saw him.

Actually, if I had only heard the voice, overheard the exchanges with the stressed-out passengers, and never even met the man I would still be telling the story to my managers of how in the midst of chaos, enthusiasm and positivity can still shine through. Meeting him was just the bonus!

It was a voice bellowing out instructions and answering questions, stern, empathetic and playful. It was on foot, moving around and restless and never sounded rehearsed or rote. It felt like this person was in the thick of it with the thousands of other stranded passengers, and he couldn't promise it would all work out rosy, but he'd be right there with us to get through. At every turn someone greeted him with a sarcastic tone or angry body language, with a dark cloud over their head, but it was like he fed off the negativity and turned it into positivity. He just kept getting stronger when most folks would have been worn down.

This is about how we met, so of course somehow, he made it over in my direction. He looked me up and down and said, "Nice suit." I said "thanks." He said, "Nice suit, but your body language says you're not feeling great about yourself." I said "yeah, it's been a rough day." Then I caught myself, felt self-conscious because this man was in the midst of some stuff! "But nothing as bad as your day." And he looked me in the eye, and smiled, and spread his arms out and said "This? This is a great day, my man." Over the course of the next year, if I had only heard second hand about the encounters and happenings in JJ's life, I would have been skeptical of the truth. But lucky for me, I had the chance to witness some things firsthand. Somehow, I had a flash of insight, though it made no sense, to invite JJ up to Boston to speak to my management team, about 60 folks. I had no idea if J could speak to a group, and we never discussed what he would say. When I gently floated the idea out there, that once in a while we got the management team together, and I need to coordinate a few things, and I wasn't sure I could even make it happen, but would he consider coming up and speaking to the group? In typical JJ fashion, he would love to come up and he was free a week from the day.

In a way, I had always looked at it like I took a chance on this stranger, based on a chance encounter, and I pat myself on the back for seeing something that many others would have missed. It's only become clear to me over time spent with Jermaine that I have it wrong. He took a chance on me, the same way he takes chances with so many people, from the homeless on the streets, to the second graders, to the strangers passing through Penn. The real gift he has, when you meet him, when you hear him speak, is he makes you feel more human and hopeful, because what you feel, feels personal and self-discovered. Later, you find out most others felt it too.

The important thing is to be accepting of failures along the way and be generous with self-forgiveness. As Jermaine says, a setback is just a setup for your comeback. It's easy to say, but living an open-hearted life means that people are going to let you down, and you're going to let yourself down. We're human. Jermaine looks like he has an infinite supply of energy and determination, but even he, I suspect, gets bogged down with self-doubt. I know I do. And when it happens you can't be too hard on yourself. I admire Jermaine's commitment to the gym. I love how he gets such a kick out of his three daughters. I think routine and humor are two things that keep our daily challenges in perspective.

If given the opportunity, I would, absolutely, do it all again, and I hope I get to do it again real soon. The response from my team was overwhelming. They are true hospitality professionals, but like a lot of young people, don't take to lecturing or preaching. Jermaine made each of them feel like he was speaking to them directly. He is a true connector. Somehow while the message is broad, the stories feel intimate and personal and truly relatable. Jermaine also is able to make it feel like a conversation.

It's not a stiff presentation, he speaks in an extemporaneous style. There's something about that

that lets people let down their guard and open up to J's insights.

Jermaine has given me clarity on something that I wrestled with--that a life of service and sacrifice can actually be restorative and energizing, not exhausting. I had seen examples with my own life, how sometimes in a grueling stretch at the restaurant, with things not going right, I was uplifted and charged up, but then in moments of achievement and satisfaction, I felt like I was carrying a heavy burden. J has such a bright energy and his service in the community and the chaos of Penn Station only seem to recharge his will and spirit. It's an amazing life lesson.

Why Jermaine?

Renee Evelyn

I first met Jermaine when he was the presenter at a male youth conference of one of my organizations. Two years later, he was the keynote speaker at the same conference which was entitled "Male by Birth, Man by Choice" with a target audience of males, ages 13-17. When the organizers thought of the person to invite to speak on that title, there was no other choice but Jermaine. His story was/is amazing and hearing it caused many emotions for attendees, especially myself, after recently giving birth to my only son. Understanding the impact that men such as Jermaine could have on my son was very eye-opening for me.

Jermaine and I remained in touch after that conference. One of the first impressions I had of Jermaine was his honesty. He is a man of his word and strives to always be open about his life in hopes that his story would reach someone. I decided I would support him on any journey he travelled because he would never take the journey without ensuring every stop made a positive impact.

Anyone seeking to achieve the peace within that Jermaine has would require much self-reflection and assessment. I'm sure for him that wasn't easy, but necessary.

Internal honesty is a must and may require taking time away from those around you. We are no good for anyone else, if we are not good for ourselves. To be able to hold someone up, we must overcome our own past deficits and struggles. Jermaine is an example of that and serves as a mentor to the young and old, providing guidance on "how to" without judgment.

Meeting Jermaine Jones has affirmed for me that will power and drive can only make one stronger, if the determination is there. There hasn't been a day that I have regretted having encountered him and I will continue to follow him because I know his journey will always be enlightening and rich with substance. Jermaine is filled with integrity, and one thing I can say I have learned from him is to never forget where you came from and who helped you along the way. His path is one to follow and anyone who meets him should be encouraged by his tell all tale.

Why Jermaine?

Aysh-sha Morgano

Jermaine and I met 25 years ago at DHL. Jermaine was a new hire, young and eager to accomplish his task at hand. I was asked to meet the new driver with a substantial amount of work in Secaucus, NJ. The initial introduction was very comical, and has been ever since our first encounter. His personality was way over the top, but very endearing. I knew from that very first day, Jermaine would remain in my life forever. His personality had all the attributes of a trustworthy friend.

Jermaine has inspired me to become a better me, always pushing me to reach my higher limit. Every text, every phone call, always came at the right time. Jermaine has a gift without even realizing it. Jermaine comes into people's lives with a purpose and changes them "one life at a time." Jermaine makes a person feel like there is hope.

During the course of our friendship, we have grown closer than family and shared all our moments and secrets. Jermaine has always been by my side. We've laughed, cried and most of all, encouraged one other throughout the difficult times we've faced in life. "I would rather walk with a friend in the dark, than alone in the light." Helen Keller

I knew Jermaine was different than the average person and I recognized his desire to push himself further. God had a plan for Jermaine, he just needed the right resources to shine through; his encouragement is beyond astonishing. Jermaine isn't afraid to share his story; his story began when he reached his lowest point in life - after pushing through his hardship moments, questioning and not receiving the answers he was looking for, but never giving up even when he wanted to at times. Once he received his breakthrough with Amtrak, he was unstoppable. God's plans were reaching his surface, and his gifts kept shining through. Jermaine gives all his credit to others. "Your Breakdown is a breakthrough." Andrea Benito

Jermaine's heart is in everything he does. God gave him this platform to share his insight on life and his life experiences to help guide someone who's going through something similar. Jermaine's perfect quote is "if I can change one person, my job is done." He has the tenacity to help others in a way people can't even imagine. He has the qualities of a great leader; his accolades speak volumes. Jermaine has accomplished so much within a short amount of time and this is just the beginning. So, if you want to follow in his footsteps, you would definitely have some big shoes to fill. "I am only one, but still I am one. I cannot do everything, but I can do something. And because I cannot do everything, I will not refuse to do the something that I can do." — Edward Everett Hale

Jermaine has taught me to live and be true to myself, be consistent with positive thoughts, be proactive with everyday living, while being committed to growing within myself and discovering my purpose in life. Jermaine will always have a positive impact on my outlook on life, and I will be forever grateful. "You can never have an impact on society if you have not changed yourself." Nelson Mandela

Why Jermaine? He is an extraordinary man; a true friend.

Why Jermaine?

Tashfia Hasan

Coordinator of Community Impact

The United Way of Harrisonburg & Rockingham County

I first met Jermaine at Penn Station where my colleague and I were eagerly and anxiously (depending on which one of us you ask) waiting for our train back to Virginia. Some fellow travelers near us seemed to have an in with one of the Amtrak employees (an interaction that was initiated by the employee) and we felt like we need to be "in" too. It was almost like they were picked to get special information about their train before it was publicized and after listening in a little more, we learned that these travelers were waiting for the same train that we were. After getting us in line before other travelers knew which platform our train would be coming to, we watched this Amtrak employee crack jokes and create a fun environment in an otherwise anxious and daunting place. He even had incredible one-liners that were great life lessons and we couldn't help but listen to him. As travelers coming back from a conference ourselves, it was extra entertaining and thought-provoking to hear this man crack jokes about how "all of these people go to conferences about lifting people up and inspiring their employees but then get to the office on Monday and drink out of a mug that tells people not to talk to them until they've had their coffee. There goes lifting people up and everything you learned at your conference!" It was a dose of realness from a stranger that was invigorating, eye-opening and challenged me to do a little better with everything I had learned in the days prior to this interaction. I was given the tools to do

110

better and with a little nudge from a stranger named Jermaine, I was excited to do better.

As I am given the privilege to learn more about Jermaine, I'm filled with curiosity. Someone who has experienced seemingly high highs and low lows still has an attitude about life that I envy but challenge myself to reflect on and learn from frequently. I'm curious: how does someone maintain a realness and optimism like Jermaine does?

How do I incorporate what he's generous to share with the world around him into my bones in a way that no matter where I am, what I'm doing or who I'm surrounded by, everything I do comes from a genuine and optimistic place? I've learned a lot but I have a lot more to learn from Jermaine.

How does anyone experience Jermaine, whether the way I did or otherwise, and not support him?! His authenticity to his own experiences and using that to fuel his energy for change in his communities and well beyond them are nothing short of inspiring to me. I have lots of days when the work seems overwhelming, when it feels like my community is screaming out for support in ways that I can't make happen quickly enough but having a light like Jermaine is the anchor that I've needed. It's been incredible the way that knowing someone like Jermaine has grounded me on the tough days. Even though my interactions with him have been limited, his impact on the way I interact with the world around me has been boundless. I have no choice but to support someone who's given me so much in so little time.

Advice for someone looking to follow Jermaine's path is soak in the world around you. Then take a step back to reflect on what lessons and opportunities you can find in those experiences. There seems to be something to be learned from every experience that life has to offer.

Reflecting on these questions has made me realize that Jermaine reinforced my need to be grounded. The world, and its needs, can feel pretty overwhelming and I'm not always in a state of mind where I can force myself to see the positive. The thing that helps me get there is to ground myself. Whether through hearing stories like Jermaine's or just taking a breath, if I can just ground myself, I can usually give my mind the break it needs to find the positive and productive. Jermaine, thank you for the reminder to stay grounded.

Why Jermaine?

Matt Falkenstein
Building & Bridge Mechanic

I first met Jermaine when I transferred into the Newark Baggage department for Amtrak. Right away, I knew Jermaine was different. At the time, I was pretty new so I wasn't looking to make any waves, I just wanted to do my job and blend in. Anybody that knows Jay, knows that he doesn't exactly blend in. But that's exactly what caught my attention.

Over time, I realized I wanted to be around him more and more because his positive attitude and work ethic was contagious. I didn't know exactly what my future held, but I knew I wanted to have the same passion that Jermaine possessed towards his job and personal projects.

Once he explained that he was looking to start up Brothers Making A Difference, I knew I wanted to be involved. Personally, I didn't have any experience with that type of program so I wasn't really sure how I could contribute, but Jay took a chance with me and enlisted me to help with a logo and any graphic design that was

needed. Truthfully, that was a big growing moment for me, because until then, I was really only designing for personal projects. But now, I had a way to contribute, and once I shared some logo ideas with Jay, I knew I had the right support and confidence from him to grow as a designer and help his vision come true.

Over the years, Jay and I have taken different paths through life, but I will always take away a valuable lesson from the experience. No matter what you pursue in life, do it with passion. Don't let fear hold you back. If you show up and work on it day after day, you will make progress. My experience with Jay was invaluable, and you can bet I would do it all over in a heartbeat. With my future in front of me, I will continue to take new adventures in life, unabashed, always remembering what I learned from Jay...CONSISTENCY IS KEY!

Why Jermaine?

Kelsey Oliveira
Student

My first encounter with Jermaine Jones was through a community service opportunity offered to me through the AmeriCorps program. This was my very first time completing such an impactful community service project like this one. Jermaine and the team, known as "Brothers Making a Difference", went to Penn Station in Newark to feed the less fortunate every week. Not only was the service I completed inspiring, but so was Jermaine. Every time we met, he had the most positive, and inspiring words to say. Mr. Jermaine made me feel like I had a new family! And although we had just met, I truly felt like I had found my place. He welcomed me, along with other members with open arms, always!

Jermaine taught me amazing things. Not only did he teach me to do better for my community, but he also stressed the importance and significance of teamwork, and that is something I will never forget. I remember each time we would meet to feed the less fortunate, Mr. Jermaine would always say at that beginning and end of our day, "Team work makes the dream work." Till this day, that is something I constantly repeat, and now use to spread the importance to others around me. Currently, I am an after-school program counselor, and a Girl Scout leader. I am constantly telling my own students about the importance of teamwork, and how far we can get when we work with our peers. I often times bring up examples that Mr. Jermaine used to tell us, and the students are always glad to hear them. I was never a person who felt completely comfortable working with others; I often times felt scared and shy to do so. Jermaine changed that entire outlook for me. Teamwork is number one, and you must be willing to work well with others in order to make the DREAM WORK.

Through my multiple encounters with Jermaine, I knew that he was a person I wanted to constantly support. Jermaine served as a mentor to me and I know that I can turn to him if I ever needed any advice. He showed me that he was truly all about helping others and wants the best for all those whom he encounters. Finding a person like Jermaine, is truly a blessing. Every day, I am thankful for all the experiences and opportunities Jermaine has given me. He is very much appreciated by all those who he encounters. I will forever be grateful for the wonderful things Jermaine has taught me. This world is lucky to have Jermaine Jones! After all, "Teamwork makes the dream work," and I am glad to be on Jermaine's team!

Why Jermaine?

Joseph J. Kranz, PhD
Managing Member, Create a Better Life LLC

The Northeast Regional Amtrak train connects New York City with cities to the north including Providence, Rhode Island. Not far out of New York, our train stalled.

Everyone was getting antsy. Then through the door burst a bright happy face. To say this Conductor was enthusiastic is a withering understatement. He proceeded to tell some jokes and pass out cardboard Conductor hats to all of the children. I stopped him and said, "Where is my hat?" He immediately gave me one, with a laugh and physical animation and said that he had overlooked that even adults like to have child- like humor sometimes. We laughed; it started a brief discussion. He said that he was new on Amtrak and that he was really enjoying his job. He had not had a job for some time, and actually had received a promotion to Junior Conductor from baggage handler. He was cheerful, powerfully happy and wonderfully helpful to our moods. He made sitting in a hot stuffy stalled car into virtually a vacation on the beach. My wife and I remarked at what a wonderful example he was as a human being who truly enjoyed other people. This man and I talked a bit about who we were and what we wanted to do in life. His dream was to start a mentoring program for inner city teenagers, and to become a motivational speaker to help other folks bring themselves up in life. Since I was familiar with how to set up organizations and get them funded, I suggested to him that we should get together and talk about how he might he be able to realize that dream. We exchanged information and began an enduring friendship which I have enjoyed for almost 10 years now. That enthusiastic Amtrak conductor is now a Station Manager for New York's Pennsylvania Station and is a motivational speaker to audiences that number thousands of people. As of 2019, Jermaine has had a highly successful inner-city mentoring program in New Jersey for over seven years. He is an absolutely amazing person who is immediately likable and is persevering, patient and persistent in keeping that dream. He is Jermaine J. (Jay) Jones.

Since I know Jermaine so well … worked with and supported him emotionally (as he has me!), and with some guidance and having seen his remarkable emergence as a true leader who is contributing incredible value to our society, I felt I owed him the time saved, to say a few words about him. Despite his jubilant, extroverted behavior, he is a humble person and an extremely dedicated and busy, only recently recovered, workaholic.

While employed as a fully qualified train conductor and because he could predict his schedule, he was able to find time to start his dream mentoring program. He decided to call it "Brothers Making A Difference" (BMAD). The name was and is appropriate because conceptually he created a family of brothers for young men who had no or little male support. It was his intention that the program would be an officially designated charity and that the personnel would all be volunteers... no paid employees. This translates into 100% of donations to BMAD being applied to programs for the young people.

Now, as a motivational speaker he has several themes and approaches to public speaking to corporate and organizational groups. He uses several uplifting themes and integrates an organization's core message, their vision, their values or specific personnel related topics. His primary approach is to humorously describe his life's journey from undereducated inner-city kid to out-of-work husband and father to NOW living his dreams. Some bylines he uses include: "Teamwork Makes the Dream Work." "You can't control the customer, but you CAN control yourself." "Be mindful; only think about THIS person, THIS issue... one at a time." "Go the extra mile; it's never crowded." "One life at a time."

Jermaine often says, "Through my life's journey, I have found that it is easy to be authentic. Allowing the good in everyone to blossom is at the root of everyone's happiness and success." Now, Jermaine has risen to be a Station Manager at New York's Pennsylvania station. Daily, he is responsible for the operations of the station including all customer service functions from security to baggage; he oversees many employees and facilitates the safe travel of thousands of people every day. None of

Jermaine's success happened overnight or without sustained effort. Attitude, perseverance, persistence, patience and respect for all made a big difference in his life.

Why Jermaine?

Sean Feeney

I met Jermaine working at Amtrak. One of the first memories I have of him was in the crew room in New Haven, CT. In our profession, we work with different people every day; so many different personalities. What stood out to me about Jermaine was his positivity. One of the first conversations we had was about how lucky and fortunate we were to have the job that we do. This was refreshing to me, because most of the time, the conversations I would have with people were about how bad everything was; 90% negative. Another one of my earliest memories of Jermaine was when we were working a train together leaving Boston, MA. I remember walking through the train and hearing Jermaine making an announcement over the PA system. This wasn't just a going through the motion kind of announcement, it was really upbeat. It was so upbeat that passengers were coming through the train and giving Jermaine high fives, complimenting how much they enjoyed his announcement. It was amazing to see, but not as amazing as what would follow.

There we were in New Haven, CT again on our layover. I noticed Jermaine had been reading a new book, so I asked him what he was reading. It turns out he was reading a book on how to start a non-profit. Jermaine then started telling me how much he wanted to help other people. He wanted to share that positive energy and his life experiences with others. He told me about Brothers Making a Difference. I'll never forget when he said "Sean, if I could just make a difference in one life, it will all be worth it to me". Right then and there, is when I believed in him and decided to support him in whatever way I could.

If there was someone that would want to follow in Jermaine's footsteps the first thing I would tell them is that they need to have tunnel vision. Jermaine knew what he wanted to do and no matter what negativity was thrown at him, or whatever obstacle was in his way, he just kept his focus on his goal. I would also tell them that it's going to take a lot of hard work and dedication.

Why Jermaine?

Melanie Oliveira
Graduate, Kean University

I met Jermaine Jones while completing a service project when I was a member of AmeriCorps. This service project was to help Brothers Making a Difference, which is an organization created by Jermaine Jones. This organization would feed those less fortunate, then us, once a week at Newark Penn station. Week after week, I came back to assist him and I instantly knew that he was someone that was going to be around for a long time. Mr. Jermaine instantly made me feel welcomed and safe. He helped break me out of my shell. When I began helping, I was a quiet girl that soon blossomed into this energetic person that was eager to help. This was all thanks to Jermaine. He makes everyone feel like they are a part of a family, like they belong.

His words of wisdom are some that I will never forget. I am currently a senior at Kean University, double majoring in Psychology and Community Recreation. In addition to being a full time student, I am also a Peer Mentor, Resident Assistant and Senator for the senior class. Whenever times get rough, or I feel overwhelmed, I remember some of the advice Jermaine used to give me. His words are something that are almost impossible to forget.

Over time, I knew Jermaine was someone that was put into my life for a reason. Hearing the motivational speeches he gave to the youth, having him always remind me to never give up, and always having someone I know I could turn to for that extra push is definitely something I would never trade.

Jermaine is the true definition of putting others before yourself. He is not selfish and is always thinking of new ways to motivate and inspire others. I will always support Jermaine and all the efforts he puts in to make a difference. Anyone that has the opportunity to meet him is very lucky and blessed to have him in their life. Jermaine had to overcome many obstacles within his life, but he never allowed that to discourage him or steer him away from his dreams. Anyone that wants to follow a similar path to Jermaine should do so with pride. Following in his footsteps is an honor.

I do not regret meeting Jermaine. I am thankful every day that I had the wonderful opportunity to meet him, work with him, and have him to guide me through life. He has shown me and taught me many lessons that I will hold close to my heart forever. I appreciate all of his efforts to make a difference and change the lives of people.

Jermaine Jones is truly an amazing individual and I am blessed to know him.

Why Jermaine?

Onique McFarlane

One of the most interesting encounters that I have had the pleasure of having was with my mentor and friend Jermaine Jones. When thinking about how we first meet, I have to say that it had to be the divine hand of God bringing our paths to cross. This encounter was totally out of my plans; I usually would never want to drink coffee after five p.m. but yet I found myself driving to Panera Bread to get a cup. After arriving and receiving my coffee, I proceeded to prep it with sugar and milk and immediately head straight for the door. Suddenly I was stopped by a gentleman who walked up to me and asked, "have you ever thought about mentoring or mentorship?" In my mind, I started to say here we go again, someone trying to sell some fake stuff. The gentleman then proceeded to try to tell me about his mentorship program, but I just wanted to leave. I then began to think maybe if I started talking about God, he will run off and leave me alone, which usually works. In this case, that plan did not work. After telling the gentleman Jesus is my mentor, he then quoted two scriptures and I then realized we both were here for a reason, the question was why?

Overtime, after randomly meeting Jermaine at various places, I finally decided to check out his program. I chose to attend a mentor/mentee meeting he was providing at a youth center not too far from where I lived. After seeing how Jermaine was treating the kids, and how the kid's demeanor changed the moment he entered the room, I then knew that

Jermaine was the real deal, and what he spoke, he backed up with actions. Suddenly things changed; the youth center and the program that they provided closed, leaving the kids who Jermaine would mentor without help - undoing the work the Jermaine and the others provided. This did not stop Jermaine, he would later founded Brothers Making a Difference; going out on his own to keep the promise he made to God years ago, which was to start an organization to help one person. Based on this concept, I have personally seen Jermaine surpass this goal on multiple occasions and I finally came to a conclusion - why ask why? As the years passed, the organization took a life of its own, and has grown to lengths only few can proclaim having a nonprofit organization.

From the perspective of someone who has been one of the original BMAD members and seeing Jermaine start from scratch, to where he is now, the only advice I would personally give to someone attempting to follow in his path is to be totally selfless. The lengths and sacrifice I have seen Jermaine personally take to keep BMAD running are unheard of. Jermaine sacrifices his own personal time, money and personal goods to keep the dream going, and in return, the efforts that he has put in has been returned to him tenfold. It takes a special person to want to help those in need without looking for anything in return from them. I have personally seen and heard of others starting their own organization, but their hearts were not in the right place, and thus failed in their endeavors. If given the opportunity, I would do it all again without question. Since I've been around Jermaine, I have improved as a person and have success in various parts of my life that we're lacking before. One of the most things important things I have learned from Jermaine was one his famous quotes "Never look down on a man, unless you are going to pick him up." A lot of the times we all judge people. We never ask ourselves what happened, or how can I help you out of this situation, instead we look down and judge, thinking that whatever situation the next person is in could never happen to us. This is the wrong; we all should be aware that no situation is uncommon to man and whatever situation the next person is in, can also happen to us without notice.

Why Jermaine?

Najah Ford

Why Jermaine Jones? Mr. Jones is not only a great friend; he is a brilliant man. He came from humble beginnings and did not allow his past to determine his future. His struggles have motivated him to be great. He has a great gift that not many people possess. Mr. Jones's gift is his ability to interact with people and motivate them. He can walk up to a stranger and have a hour long meaningful conversation. His personality is contagious, and he brings joy to everyone he meets.

His journey through life is amazing, and he tells his story so well that you could picture yourself being by his side every step of the way. He is a man of integrity. He does what he says he will do and has an unmatched level of loyalty. Why Jermaine Jones? He is one of a kind and he is just in the beginning stages of changing many people's lives for the better with his words of wisdom!!!

Why Jermaine?

Ty Page

One beautiful summer evening, while traveling from work and reflecting on my day, a conversation occurred between myself and a few other passengers regarding the consistency of a father's presence in the home. This particular evening, the light rail was unusually overcrowded. After undergoing a stressful day at work, I didn't want to partake in the conversation, but the topic piqued my interest and I also enjoy conversing with people. Therefore, I could not resist. As the train came to my stop, I proceeded to exit and a gentleman from that group of passengers approached me. He introduced himself as Jermaine Jones and complimented me on my positive demeanor on the topic of our conversation. He then took notice that I had a rough day but was impressed with the way I handled myself to where it was undetectable.

Jermaine also stated he had been observing my pleasant interactions with other fellow passengers on numerous occasions where my reality did not reflect my actions. We then shifted our conversation on Christianity. He then stated his now famous mottos: "consistency is key", "do your job above and beyond because you never know who you will run into." And my favorite, "don't look down on a man unless you're reaching out your hand to lift him up". We then stood on the corner for an hour and a half talking about an array of topics. He then stopped and looked up to the sky and repeated "I hear you father" and begun to minister to me, "I know you have been going through some rough times, but through it you have never let anyone see it. I am going to be obedient to the father." He then urged me to apply for a job with his employer, Amtrak, where he confirmed I would be employed there within two months. Jermaine's exact words were manifested on September 11, 2012, which he changed my life forever, and I am extremely grateful that the Most High aligned us to cross paths.

Over the course of a few months, I expressed my altruistic interest in helping people who are in need. There, Jermaine introduced me to his nonprofit organization, Brothers Making A Difference. He then invited me to feed the homeless in downtown Newark, NJ. It was an awesome experience giving back to our community. I knew Jermaine had a big heart, but his actions solidified it for me. He continued to be selfless and always give 110% of himself by giving back to those less fortunate. I decided to join Jermaine's organization because of his selfless endeavors, but most importantly, leading by examples. He doesn't just talk; he is about actions and putting forth the work and grind. If anyone wants to start their own nonprofit, I would definitely recommend Jermaine. He has a people first attitude, an overachiever work ethic, first impression is key attitude, a relentless can-do attitude. Working with Jermaine has been a fulfilling journey; using his principles and "consistency is key" phrase has provided me with great success as a husband,

father, son, brother and friend. I envisioned much
success in his future endeavors and blessings to my
big brother, Jermaine Jones.

Why Jermaine?

Robin Miller

It was the of Summer 2017. My 8 and 10 year old daughters had just spent their first night in NYC. We were standing in the middle of Penn Station, in front of the arrival and departure board, waiting to see what track our train would be on. We were early since we had checked out of our hotel. Since we come from an incredibly small remote ski town in Colorado, I was playing the role of protective Mother Hen. Constantly looking around to make sure we were safe. It was crowded and hectic. Suddenly, this man came up to us and started to announce, over and over, to the people around us, "VIPs people!!! No pictures please!!!" He was waving his hands as if to keep people from trying to get our autographs. The girls and I looked at each other in confusion. What is this man doing???? He introduced himself, with a large smile, as Jermaine Jones, the manager of Penn Station. He welcomed us and then went to get the girls some crayons and coloring books. We just started laughing. My fear was washed away. I felt safe in this huge crowd of strangers. We have been friends with Jermaine ever since.

He gave us his card and said if we ever came through again, to let him know. We have seen Jermaine every summer visit since.

Jermaine is an inspiration to me. He works so hard at his "paid job," and then works harder to advance the non-profit, BMAD, which he started. We are in contact about once a week through text. We send

141

each other notes about accomplishments or inspirational quotes.

I wish the world had more people like Jermaine. He understands the philosophy that by giving, you receive. It's not about material things but being connected to humanity. I am a recovering Alcoholic. I am a member of a 12-step program which is based on service. We cannot keep what we have unless we give it away. I was given guidance and I in turn give guidance to those just coming into the program. Jermaine lives his life in the same way. He inspires me.

My advice to someone who wants to follow a similar path to Jermaine's is to find a way to help others. We all have experience with something that we need others to support. If we all look outside ourselves, we can find a path. I only wish I lived closer and could be more connected to Jermaine. It would be an honor to work closely with him.

Jermaine's moto, "never stop believing in yourself" has had a huge impact on me. I think we all have periods of self-doubt and confusion. I can always hear Jermaine saying this. I think to myself, if he can do it, with everything on his plate, so can I. I can also pass this along to those I am trying to help.

Why Jermaine?

Emily Gafanhao

"Consistency is Key!" Mr. Jermaine Jones has been one of the most inspiring people I've had the opportunity to meet. I remember sitting through his speech as he took us through an emotional journey that is his life. His highs and lows and then his highs again. He mentioned his goals and his dreams, and I knew in that moment, this man was the epitome of the words "consistency is key."

I started volunteering for Brothers Making a Difference shortly after meeting Mr. Jermaine (the same day as a matter of fact) because I knew he was onto something great. I remember standing behind those tables and watching as dozens of homeless people ran to find their place in the line in hopes of getting a warm meal for the night. Watching as Mr. Jermaine stood there, with awe in his eyes, I could sense his pride and gratefulness in his work, and in his friends that took the time to help him accomplish his goals

Mr. Jermaine is a kind, caring and overall inspiring man. He has overcome, and will continue to do so, because I know one thing for sure, "consistency is key!"

Why Jermaine?

Susan Pope
CEO, I Dance Because

I first meant Jermaine Jones at the Essex County Youth House when he came to facilitate a workshop for incarcerated youth. The program was a part of my sororities E.M.B.O.D.I. (Empowering Males to Build Opportunities for Independence) program. Our boys were a tough audience, but Jermaine had them fully engaged. I was immediately amazed at how sincere, charismatic and authentic Jermaine was. I knew from that moment on that I wanted to be able to capture an audience like that. It wasn't just that he had the boy's attention; he was telling his story which could possibly serve as a template for their success. Jermaine came to be one of our featured facilitators for our E.M.B.O.D.I. program. A couple of years after that first meeting, we asked Jermaine to be our keynote speaker for our E.M.B.O.D.I. conference which serviced over 500 men and boys from the community. He delivered a keynote address that was inspiring and motivating.

Over time, I continued to follow Jermaine's career, taking notes along the way. I accepted an invitation to volunteer for his organization Brother's Making a Difference by feeding the homeless at Newark Penn Station. I have been involved in volunteer opportunities before, but this one was different. This opportunity gave me the chance get close and personal with the homeless population in a way I had never experienced. Again, I realized I needed to learn as much as I could from Jermaine. I believed in his mission and decided to support his efforts.

Fast forward a couple of years, I started my own non-profit organization I DANCE BECAUSE to help aspiring dancers with scholarships and to celebrate the positive and effective way dance changes one's life for the better. Jermaine has been a faithful supporter of my organization. His support has helped me believe in what I'm doing and continue to push forward even when it is difficult. My advice for anyone who wants to follow a similar path to Jermaine's is to first believe in what you are doing. Second, take notes along the way. Jermaine is passionate about what he does, and it is evident in his work.

If I had the opportunity to support, or not support Jermaine again, I definitely would support. Having his business model as an example has truly helped me to see the light at the end of tunnel. Even when I can't see the light, I believe it's there. I am always inspired by any chance meetings we have. Just when I start to get discouraged, I get an email or text from Jermaine pushing me forward. Jermaine Jones is the real deal in success stories. The one thing I have learned from Jermaine is to never, never give up. I dance because God has called me to help others heal through the power of dance.

The only thing I cannot do is fail.

Why Jermaine?

Neil Padden
Senior Vice President of Sales

I imagine my first encounter with Jermaine Jones is similar to many people – and I am sure the same sentence can be written over and over: "I was traveling through Penn Station with my Family. I was tired, a bit frazzled and in need of some guidance. I had my family counting on me to get them through this maze of people.

As I stood there in the middle of Penn Station looking a bit confused, a man in a suit with a commanding voice said to me "Brother, it looks like you can use some help – how can I be of service to you?" What? Let me remind you – I am in in the middle of Penn Station – like standing inside a beehive with so much activity around me, that it is a challenge to focus. Jermaine's booming voice cut through the air and he assured me that we were in good hands and he would help us navigate to our Train.

When I think back to that time, it was as though Jermaine had a keen focus – but his focus was centered on isolating issues or potential problems. He locked onto our family as a group that needed assistance – and he immediately went into action.

After our meeting, I explained our encounter with Jermaine and his team at Penn Station to my extended family. My mother said, "I know this is not the last time you will hear about this man Jermaine Jones." I agreed! I was so impressed with his "Above and Beyond Service" that I wrote a letter to the CEO of Amtrak (which I understand is not all that uncommon for someone to remember and call out Jermaine for his over- the-top service!)

It was only after we met Jermaine the first time in Penn Station that I found out about his other passion: Brothers Making a Difference. Not only does Jermaine go above and beyond at his "day job" – but he has another dedication that also is an example of Jermaine giving of himself to help others.

I wish I could say that I support Jermaine- but it is the other way around. As a busy professional, I am in and out of airports, hotels and meetings on a constant basis. I look forward to the weekly text from Jermaine with inspirational pictures, quotes and testimonials. He supports me! He inspires me! I am not the focus of the efforts of Brothers Making a Difference- but I am certainly a beneficiary of his good work!

Initially, one might say Jermaine does not have a unique story. Everyone has personal issues. We all can say that we have had concerns with our careers or finding the right job – or even depression. But what makes Jermaine magical is his ability to see through those issues and concerns – and to make others around him see through their issues, to show the positive outcome that is possible. His ability to provide his own testimonial is at the core of his magic. I listen to Jermaine because he is authentic – he is real. My advice to those who want to be like Jermaine. Be real – Face your fears - Chase your dreams – Never (Ever) Quit.

He always (ALWAYS!) reminds me that in the beginning, he would drive a few hours just to speak to a few people. He says "one life at a time" – to Jermaine this is not a T- shirt slogan or some branding gimmick – He believes this to be a simple truth! Meeting Jermaine is a highlight in my life. If you have not met Jermaine- you will understand what I mean after you spend some time with this man. I talk about him often to others. I remain inspired by him as I think about my own personal life and professional future.

I received a call recently from a good friend – and former business associate. He said, "I am going to mention a name to you that we both have in common and you are never going to guess who it is?" I did not try to guess - but when he threw out the name Jermaine Jones – I was speechless. At first, I thought, "maybe I am not so special that Jermaine picked me out of the crowd at Penn Station to help only me." Then, I relished in the fact that my friend had the EXACT same experience that I had at Penn Station and has continued to build a relationship with Jermaine like I have. I realized at that point that Jermaine's reach is broad – and his message resonates with everyone! His impact is hard to measure but below are a few points that resonate from my time around Jermaine:

- Never Quit. If anyone should have quit, it would have been Jermaine. The story of his personal and professional challenges are real – but his determination is stronger that the negatives pressures that he faces. His favorite line "when you think about quitting – think about why you started."

- One Life at a Time: There was a time when Jermaine did not have an auditorium filled with people. He often tells me that he would be happy to drive for a few hours to speak to one or two people about his experiences or "Brothers Making a Difference."

- Create your own magic: All of the activity that you see with Jermaine is his own doing. His career, accolades, etc.

- Make a Difference: Jermaine "makes a difference" in his day job at Amtrak helping people like me. But I also noticed something further as I spent more and more time around Jermaine at Penn Station – he teaches others around him at Penn Station to do the same thing. He has created a culture of those who act like him. Everyone that I encountered at Penn who works with Jermaine has developed this sense of understanding about Customer Service.

Jermaine's philanthropy: Brothers Making a Difference is built upon the simple premise of helping others. This is a theme that Jermaine threads into the fabric of his life.

Why Jermaine?

Ariel Givens

I met Jermaine quite a few years ago at a bowling alley. It was impossible not to notice him. He was the loudest person in the bowling alley. I typically steer clear of these types of people, but I'm glad I got to know him. Once you get to know Jermaine, you realize that he is extremely down to earth and friendly. Jermaine has always been the type of person dedicated to giving back to his community. I was excited when he began organizing prepared food donations outside of Newark Penn Station. He didn't ask for anything other than your support. Over the months/years, it was great to see the groups of volunteers grow from local individuals to corporate volunteers. The people we served were always grateful and looked forward to seeing us each week.

For anyone looking to follow the same path that Jermaine has taken, I would suggest that they never give up. I would suggest that they view all of their obstacles as opportunities to grow. I would also suggest that they treat everyone equally. The true character of a person shines the brightest when you see how they treat someone who doesn't have much to offer them.

I truly value the friendship that I've developed with Jermaine. Watching him interact with others has definitely made me a better person. I've learned from Jermaine to understand that behind every person is a story that is most likely not similar to mine. I've learned to respect everyone's differences and take the time to hear everyone's story. I've learned that you receive the most valuable gifts from those who don't have much to offer you.

Why Jermaine?

Alyssa Radigan
School Counselor

I met Jermaine Jones at my school's Career Day in January 2015. Jermaine walked in and had this big, infectious smile on his face. We instantly connected and talked for about 15 minutes prior to the start of the day's events. We then picked up our conversation at the conclusion of this wonderful day! I felt anxious and nervous for my first Career Day and Jermaine, unknowingly, calmed my nerves and helped me change my mindset to feeling excited to conquer the day. This is the exact effect that he has on people. He motivates and inspires them. Each time I open up a friendly email from him, or he walks into our school building, I get so excited to reconnect with him.

Jermaine has made it a point to come to my school at least once a year, and our students, and myself, look forward to seeing him and listening to his message each and every time.

Jermaine instantly became a part of the Roosevelt School family from the moment he entered our building in 2015. I feel pure happiness knowing that Jermaine is a part of my life and my students' lives. He inspires us all and motivates us to be better people.

Supporting Jermaine was a no-brainer for me. It is the least I can do since he is the true supporter. The way he supports our students and faculty is admirable. So, supporting him is not even a question! His story and message are uplifting and gives us all hope and the desire to want to do and be better.

If someone wants to follow in a similar path, I would advise them to DOT IT and not give up. I want to quote Jermaine here and say that they need to have "energy, a positive attitude and be consistent!" Those three characteristics will help them succeed and reach their goals and dreams.

I couldn't be happier or more grateful that Jermaine and I have crossed paths in this lifetime. I would meet him 100 times over again, and I would invite him into our family 100 times over again. His contagious energy and outlook on life are rare. There are not many people out there who have his type of influence on every person they meet.

I'm going to quote Jermaine again, "Energy. Attitude. Consistency." These three powerful words that Jermaine uses to teach our staff and students are the words that I need to play on repeat for myself and for my students. They are three words that can be applied to all aspects of a person's life. I have been going through a difficult time lately, and when Jermaine preached about these three words at my school, they really resonated with me. They were what I needed to hear, and I think everyone can follow them on a daily basis. Having high energy, a positive attitude and remaining consistent allows you to be the best version of yourself and achieve your goals!

Why Jermaine?

Capt. Robert Smith

Jermaine Jones and I first met back in 2010 at Newark Penn Station in New Jersey soon after he was hired as a baggage man for Amtrak. As an Amtrak Police Sergeant one of my duties was to conduct platform patrols and to protect our customers and employees, so I got to spend lots of time in his presence. Whenever Jermaine Jones was working, the one thing I immediately noticed was Jermaine's profound skill to empathize with customers and to leave everyone he helped out with a smile. He was clearly a customer service leader in both his words and in his actions. No matter what mode of transportation you use, traveling can be extremely stressful and confusing. In general, rail passengers want to be on time for their train, they want to know they're on the correct platform and that they are boarding the correct train. I saw how Jermaine could take charge of a crowded platform full of passengers and quickly guide and calm everyone so they could board the right train quickly and safely. Jermaine was and remains gifted at putting customers first, making them feel important and reducing the overall stress of their travel. I often told him, you are going places at Amtrak and any other company that is fortunate enough to hire you. I said that he was going to be a Vice President, or higher, at Amtrak someday because of the way in which he treated our customers. I knew he was a genuinely good, caring man with a larger than life personality.

My relationship with Jermaine has grown stronger over the past 10 years. He shared wonderful stories about his parents and how they taught him about love, survival, hard work and respect for his fellow man. Jermaine has a strong faith in God that he quietly shows through his actions. I remember when he became a Conductor on the very busy Northeast Corridor between New York and Washington. When Jermaine became a Customer Service Manager in the New York Division, I knew he truly earned the position through his consistency and actions. He maintained his consistently positive and empathetic customer care in these demanding jobs. I was so excited when he got both positions and said to him, I told you! You will keep moving up at Amtrak! Someday the president!

Last year, Jermaine was awarded Amtrak's prestigious President's Safety Award and was recognized for his efforts in customer care and safety. He was so proud and grateful that his mother was able to join him at the ceremony to witness the honor. Off- duty, Jermaine supports the youth in his community. One of his organizations is Brothers Making A Difference. Their motto is "Never look down on a man, unless you are going to pick him up."

Jermaine will always offer to help his customers, his neighbors and the downtrodden. When Jermaine told me about this writing project, I was excited to participate and honored that he asked for my input. He has a positive uplifting influence on the people he meets. He is an example of genuine customer service in both words and actions.

His positive energy is contagious. I believe in leading by example and Jermaine Jones does just that. As a Customer Service Manager, Jermaine has many responsibilities. However, he always takes the time to be out on the front line, engaging with passengers and offering to ease the stress of their travels. He has been consistent in all the years I have known him. Jermaine is a natural leader and an inspiration to both young and old. A person who wants to follow a similar path to Jermaine should understand their faith. They should practice loving one another, empathizing with others and willing to guide others on a path of goodness.

From my first encounter with Jermaine, and through today, the one thing that is very clear is that Jermaine is consistent in his positiveness and willingness to inspire the lives of others. His love of God and the love, wisdom and guidance he was given by his parents is very clear in how he works with his fellow man. Those of us who have gotten to know Jermaine are fortunate. What I've learned from Jermaine that has stayed me is that kindness is not weakness, and demanding the best from others, is not mean.

Jermaine Jones lives the words of Dr. Martin Luther King, Jr. who said, "Life's most persistent and urgent question is, What are you doing for others?"

Why Jermaine?

Darold Hall

I've known Jermaine since we were younger; he went to school with my older brother. My personal experience didn't happen until I met him at the barbershop, and I started cutting his hair. He was working for DHL; always full of energy, always positive.

Jermaine gave me a feeling of comfort, togetherness and family. Since the beginning of my career at the barbershop, he supported me and he's been supporting me ever since. Jermaine would send me referrals or would specifically have me cut his hair as a new barber, and that meant a lot to me.

I know that he is always someone I can call for any situation. He's always going to be there at the drop of a dime. It never changes, no matter what. He's always the same person - like a big brother!

I decided to support Jermaine because he's that kind of supporter with me - I had to be the same way, to return that energy. The consistency factor that Jermaine possesses is what made me support him and Brothers Making a Difference.

I would advise someone to use Jermaine as a personal coach because it's going to be hard to duplicate the person that he is without him coaching you. Everyone doesn't have the gift that he has. When he walks into a room, by the time he leaves out, you will know what he represents and that's imperative to have when it comes to leadership.

Given the opportunity, yes, I would do it all again. I would be more involved and get more mentorship from him. I would model how he does things and the way he goes about leading the youth.

The one thing I learned from Jermaine is being persistent in your lifestyle, in your goals and not giving up. You have to find a way to dig deep and pull the person that you deserve to be out of you; just as he does.

Why Jermaine?

.

Eric Rhett
Sr. Production Manager
Black Entertainment Television

When I met first met brother Jermaine it was through a mutual friend. My friend explained to me how when he met brother Jermaine, his energy was like nothing he's ever seen before. He was the loudest voice in the station, but his voice and energy lit up the atmosphere with peace, love and joy. As we approached the Amtrak station, I could hear a voice that sounded similar to how my friend described. As we got closer, the voice became more powerful and the energy began to give me goosebumps. I eventually could see and hear brother Jermaine loud and clear, "right this way folks, if you need help with your bags, no worry, I got you covered, and remember don't forget to smile, it doesn't cost you a thing." My first reaction, after I introduced myself and shook his hand, was this guy has to be acting...where are the cameras? Three years later, he's still the same guy I met on day one, and I have yet to see any cameras.

Since the day we first met, I assumed brother Jermaine's kind and loveable energy would dwindle, but to my surprise, it only got stronger. No matter the location, environment, people, gender or race, brother Jermaine continued to encourage folk, give sound advice, and constantly remind us all "don't forget to smile, it doesn't cost you a thing." He eventually became someone I could go to, or be around, whenever I needed great advice or be reminded "consistency is key."

I would say to most, if Jesus was here today, in the living flesh, brother Jermaine would come the closest to being just like him. While in my presence, I can confirm he has never taken a second off from smiling or being positive, even in the most uncomfortable situations. He's always led by example of what it takes to be the sharpest tool in the shed. I have never in my entire life, met anyone who was so dedicated and passionate about helping others on a daily basis, at no cost, than brother Jermaine.

To those interested in taking a similar path as brother Jermaine, I would give one piece of advice that he's always given me…"one life at a time." You can't change the world over night, but if you focus on changing one life at a time, you'll be surprised at how much you can accomplish over time. It can be making someone smile, giving someone a compliment, giving someone a meal, helping someone with their bags…every good deed counts.

In my field of work, I've had the privilege of being around successful men and women of all kind. However, none of them have given me the inspiration on a consistent basis like brother Jermaine…not even close. Every day I receive a text message of some sort, reminding me "consistency is key." Brother Jermaine taught me the ultimate lesson that I will cherish for the rest of my life; you don't have to be great at something to get started but you have to start in order to one day be great. I am forever thankful to have met someone like brother Jermaine.

He's the living example that if you believe it, you can be it...and don't let anyone tell you otherwise. I once asked brother Jermaine, "how do you wake every day, always ready to help others, feed the homeless, speak to thousands of people, donate money, donate time, work with kids, go to the gym...all with a smile? ...and he said, "there's never any traffic on the extra mile."

Why Jermaine?

Chris Taylor

Aneis Consulting Group

Spring 2010-

I walked in Panera Bread that morning for coffee; the line backed up to the door. "I am going to be late for my class at this rate!" Just then, a man walked up and said, "excuse me, may I ask you a question?" "Me? You are speaking to me?" I looked around and thought he meant someone else in the line because I don't know this guy!! ("Oh no, hustling has come to Montclair!"). "Yes," the fellow said, "would you look at my resume; I am applying for a job and I have an interview this afternoon." Okay, I don't have time for this; I just came to get coffee and be on my way, and I opened my mouth to say "no," but the words that came out were, "after I get my coffee, I'll come over."

So, I read his resume. I learned he had applied for countless jobs, all turned down. His dream was to be a conductor with AMTRAK, but they had turned him down as well. He had lost his job over a year ago, and with a wife and family to support; finances were whittled to zero-his anxiety and depression were mounting. With no money for clothes, he wore a donated suit that was too big for him; a shirt that was slightly dingy; a tie, slightly wrinkled, shoes he had found and no socks. Yet, after all he revealed, he said he forced himself to be optimistic!

Over the ensuing months, he made a point of coming up to me at Panera Bread (my hang out to do homework) and tell me of his progress. Interview after interview, he was turned down, until one day, there was a break. It was not what he wanted, but he accepted, still applying to AMTRAK. His dogged perseverance was a spectacle to witness until one day, ebullient and beaming, he had an appointment for an interview with the rail service. And so, started the most incredible, heart-warming, journey anyone would have the privilege to witness!

Over the next four years, I had the pleasure of witnessing a meteoric rise - from a Baggage Handler to Service Attendant to Lead Service Attendant to Conductor to Station Manager! Incredible!! Silently, I cried tears of joy at hearing every promotion. But more was to come.

In 2012, Jermaine told me he wanted to start a nonprofit for kids and asked did I have any advice. I gave a few tips and before year's end, BMAD (Brothers Making a Difference) was born. As always, he kept me informed about his progress and over the years, he grew from a struggled beginning to seeking sponsor/fundraising support to visiting schools to being a sought after motivation speaker for large corporate events. TEDX here he comes!!! It is rare to witness adult growth, that continuing quest for more, for greater, for improvement. But what is rarer is witnessing sheer determination and faith of holding intended goals in the face of obstacles. While no one can really follow the path/footprint of another, that is always up to each individual. However, one can follow the stardust left in the wake of his stellar accomplishments, and in doing so, one is able to take advantage of a supernova as it emits a light billions of times brighter than the brightest star.

2020

Everyone deserves our attention in some way because I believe we are all connected. That said, some efforts would require more of our time than others. For me, these are the qualities that stand out in Jermaine:

Risk taker; Willingness to listen and learn; Sincerity; Non-pretentious

Happy to share accomplishments and how he did it (different from empty bagging); Personable and Laser-like focus.

And so, that day at Panera Bread, Jermaine followed his heart and took a risk. From jobless and penniless, to sought after speaker and soon to be published author, it's a rare gift to see stardust left by a supernova as it passed through our lives! Only the best with your book!

Why Jermaine?

Lailah Harrigan

Entrepreneur

On May 5, 2017, I met a gentle giant, Jermaine Jones, at Amtrak Penn Station. I was travelling to Baltimore, MD, rushing so I wouldn't miss my train. It was crowded that morning and people were forming a line to get to their track departure. Gratefully, there was time, so I stood against a railing with my suitcase and was reading from my cellphone. Suddenly, I hear an Amtrak Station Manager saying, "Form a line and smile, don't be so serious." I watched him for a few minutes interacting with the passengers; some were laughing, and others were talking about this gentlemen's posture and encouragement. He truly put a smile on my face, and he escorted me over to the side, helping me with my suitcase near my track and we had great conversation. Amazing for me, because you can really see how inspiration, thoughtfulness and positive vibes can empower so many people. He's such a gentleman and had one of his workers help me with my bags onto the train. Inspired action can get the attention of a CEO of a major Fortune 500 company who believed Jermaine could inspire thousands as a Keynote Speaker.

I've always believed that positive energy and enthusiasm can create a shift in a room, and it certainly allowed us to exchange information and become great friends from one encounter. Who knew that I would gain a tremendous mentor, and friend, that gives his all in every aspect of his being? One thing for sure and two things for certain, there are no accidents in life, and everything happens as it should. I'm a big supporter, and the work he's put in with his organization, Brothers Making a Difference, is changing lives and adding value. He's a mentor, leader and an inspiration living in his greatness. The world is a better place when you let your light shine and be who you were gifted to be. We all have a divine purpose on this planet to impact the world for sure. Thank you, Jermaine, for touching so many people with you gifts and talent.

Why Jermaine?

Kenneth Earl Spinks

I first met Jermaine on 21st street in Irvington, NJ in the 80's. He was always loud; he had a burst of energy. Jermaine made you feel comfortable; he never came as a threat. He was always a down to earth brother to me. He has a message behind his words.

He's always willing to help you. I've been feeding the community on Thanksgiving for about 25 years, and I've never had to ask him would he donate to the cause, he just would!

Jermaine has always been a burst of love – he would give you the shirt off his back. He's a go-getter. Jermaine has always been there for me, even when I didn't know what I was doing. He is the one that got me to start doing comedy. He told me to check out the NYC comedy scene and I did. I had all original jokes that you never heard before. He always told me "you don't want to be on the dying bed saying I would've should've could've." I did it for about 3-4 years, then my first wife died, and I stopped.

Jermaine is a role model, minister and father-like figure. He comes into the barbershop and speaks to come of my clients from time to time. I've never seen Jermaine not smile; he always has a huge smile on his face. One day, I had on a BMAD shirt coming back from a trip, and a guy said I know him, and pointed at the shirt. Every place I go, I take shirts with me and I leave some for the people there. When he got to a point in life when he wanted to kill

178

himself, I was there. If he didn't have the money, I would let him get a free cut because a good hair cut will make you feel better, and when you feel good, you do good. He works with me because he sees the genuineness in me. "Those that do the most talking, do the least whatever." He knows I'm not just talking; I'm doing things for the community; I do Christmas, Thanksgiving, and school bookbag drives.

I know Jermaine, I see Jermaine and what he is truly doing for others. He's a person who does things from the kindness of his heart. He has a genuine love for people. Men don't go to people for help, we always just try to figure it out on our own. When I went to him about a year and a half ago, he said that I have to get away from the people who don't mean me any good. Those were powerful words. He always tells me "stay focused because the world is always watching us."

I decided to support Jermaine because I know his heart. He is a great guy. He expects respect because he gives respect. For anyone looking to do the same, I would say find your own lane and stay focused.

One last quick story. I remember one day Jermaine asked me how many kids hair can I cut on a Wednesday from 11am - 3pm. I said, "about 12-15" and he said "you meant to say 28!" I started laughing and said "yeah, I can do about 27." And we got it done in due time. Jermaine is an outstanding guy. I love him man, I really do love him.

Why Jermaine?

Thomas & Michelle Taylor

Owner, Tom Taylor Electric

Director of Operations, Syracuse University Setnor
School of Music

Jermaine is memorable. If you have met him even once, you know that. You just have to hear his booming, friendly voice once, or see his smile, his purposeful walk, and he's cemented in your mind. As he moves through his "office" the train station - greeting colleagues, helping travelers, predicting what people will ask, what they need - Jermaine is a graceful force, a welcoming, calming presence at one of the busiest spots in the country, Penn Station, NYC.

We first met him when we were taking a group of college students to New York City for the week. We were heading back home and encountered him in Penn Station. We were all tired, dreading that last big push of the trip, boarding everyone and all their stuff, knowing we would have to squeeze through crowds hauling heavy luggage, risk getting separated from the group, feeling panicked, and having our last moments in New York end in a stressed out rush.

But, no. Thanks to Jermaine, he not only kept the groups together and took care of everyone but gave the students one last - and perhaps the most lasting – talk. After hearing they were there on a career development trip, he talked about professions, success, and life. Those students had a whirlwind trip and may lose the memory of a lot of the details in time, but they will not forget Jermaine.

We look forward to seeing him every year on that trip. We know the students will be surprised, delighted, and energized by talking with him. We know our little son, who has been on the trip since he was a baby, will listen to Jermaine talk with the same spellbound attention everyone else does, looking forward to every word. Each year, when he talks with the students, it is like he connects everything they heard all week and sums it down to the most important elements – how they treat people, how they can help make a difference, and how they can make the most of their talents.

I am sure everyone has stories about him – I saw him on one of our trips quietly pull a mom aside whose child was noticeably sick, so she could get settled in early on her train. I have seen him turn in six directions, giving out information and help to people, and then not missing a minute as he checked on a staff member. I watched him give a quiet little child the chance to make a loud announcement over the speakers at the station. All without missing a beat as he helped countless people in the grand lobby.

I think it would be impossible for him not to bring that energy, knowledge, and care to everything he does - his career, volunteer work, speaking engagements, friends and family, and his work with Brothers Making a Difference.

His energy is unforgettable, but I think what surprises and sticks with me most about Jermaine is how many people he remembers. Their names, where they are from, details of their lives. He must see hundreds of people every day. Thousands and thousands of people go through that station. People working, commuting, running – people in a rush, people lost, happy, confused, sad, or scared. Who knows how many people he interacts with in a year? I can't even guess, but I do know that every one of those people leave his presence less lost, confused, or scared, and feeling lifted up just by the interaction.

I think he can remember so many people and anticipate needs so well, because he really does care about people. When he asks, "how are you doing?" he isn't just being polite. He actually wants to know, and if there is a problem – if you are not fine - he will help. He has diligently built on his experience and refined his incredible people skills, but it is more than that. He remembers people because they are important to him – he places great value on who they are, what they care about, and what they need, and sees the value and gifts in everyone. And in that way, he shares his gifts with everyone he meets.

Why Jermaine?

Tara Horniacek

I met Jermaine, aka Mr. Jones, approximately ten years ago through my dad, Tommy Horniacek, at North Arlington Bowl O Drome. My dad and Jermaine bowled together for many years and continued their friendship after Jermaine stopped bowling. I remember Jermaine working for Amtrak, and when career day came up at my school in 7th grade, my dad suggested for him to speak at my school. I also thought it was a good idea to ask Jermaine, with the position he was in at Amtrak, to also speak about his non-profit organization 'Brothers Making A Difference.' Since 2015 until present day, Jermaine continues to speak at Roosevelt School in Lyndhurst, New Jersey and many other schools when asked. I'm proud to call Jermaine my friend, and I know he will continue to do great things in the years ahead.

Why Jermaine?

Robert Sullivan
SVP of Sales & Service
The Madison Square Garden Company

It was a blazing, hot and humid NJ summer afternoon in July of 2012. My wife and I had planned a weekend away from our four children; a weekend in Boston to watch the Yankees take on the Red Sox at Fenway Park. The train time was 2pm and we are waiting on the platform with the excitement of two teenagers. Cold beers, baseball, hot dogs, no kids.... what could be better!?! The train pulled in and we could not wait to get on board. The heat and humidity were so high, we had sweat through our clothes, and we would welcome the air conditioning and comfortable seats of the Acela Train. However, the train just sat there with its doors closed. And sat

there. And sat there. Finally, there was a PA announcement that the train had lost power and would need to be fixed right there on the tracks. A collective "uhhhh" could be heard from the 100 or so customers waiting patiently on the platform to board the train. Some were headed home from work in NJ/NY, some were starting their summer vacations, while others were just like us, headed to Fenway for a weekend of rivalry baseball. And as we waited on the track, the frustration grew. The complaints grew.

Our patience grew short and we continued to wait, and sweat, and hope something could be done. And out of nowhere, a loud and distinctive voice could be heard over the crowd: "LADIES AND GENTLEMEN. ON BEHALF OF AMTRAK, WE SINCERELY APOLOGIZE FOR THE WAIT. WE KNOW YOU'RE LOOKING FORWARD TO GETTING ON THAT TRAIN

AND I PROMISE YOU, WE ARE DOING EVERTHING WE CAN TO FIX IT. IN FACT, MY MAN BRIAN IS ON THE JOB. IF ANYONE CAN FIX THIS TRAIN, IT'S BRIAN, SO WE KNOW WE HAVE THE RIGHT MAN FOR THE JOB. MY NAME IS JERMAINE AND I PROMISE TO KEEP YOU UPDATED."

It was the relief we all needed. A reassuring voice in a sea of doubt. Someone to take control and say, "I've got you." I watched as Jermaine then interacted with those waiting, telling jokes, asking questions, interacting and keeping them occupied. And then there is was, 10 minutes later, the sound of a train powering up, the doors opening, and our weekend back on track, pun intended. I introduced myself to Jermaine and told him I was an Executive with the NY Jets, and if we had a stadium full of employees like him, we'd never have to worry about the outcome of our games, knowing that our fans would still have a great time. Jermaine had a choice that day. With a platform full of angry sharks, he chose to jump in the pool. He could have easily walked down the stairs to the climate-controlled concourse and avoided the challenge. He, instead, opted to take us all on and he converted us from frustrated customers to Jermaine evangelists.

Jermaine and I have stayed in touch since that afternoon. In fact, we have become friends and trusted business partners. We have volunteered together and watched football and basketball games together with his Brothers Making a Difference volunteers. We're shared emails, text messages and hugs in Penn Station on my way to the office. I've had Jermaine come in and speak to my business team at Madison Square Garden. Jermaine has inspired me to be a better man, a better father, a better human being. There are those who take in this life and there are those who give, and everyone in-between. Jermaine is the embodiment of a giving soul. A man who makes the world a better place to live. He inspires me and many others daily with his smile, his positivity, and his relentless pursuit of selflessness. The man works harder than anyone I have known other than my father. They are cut from the same cloth, men who feel that retirement is a good time to rest, and until then, they will make the world we live in a better place to be. One person at a time. Why Jermaine? Because he makes us better. He inspires us to take less and give more. He lifts our spirits for no other gain than the smile on his face and the one we share back. Jermaine is a gift to us all, and I will forever love him because of it.

Why Jermaine?

Wil Townsend

Why Jermaine? Well almost anyone can answer this question but it's truly those that have worked closely with that man that can really tell you why him. He works hard...quietly. He just does what others won't and don't do. He's toiling away at his craft day in and day out. Why Jermaine - because people like him get busy working.

They surround themselves with positive people who build them up, not tear them down. Life is hard enough, without having to worry about negative people slowing you down. Why Jermaine? He's one of those people always building you up.

Why Jermaine? He puts positive seeds into his mind every single day. All of us wake up with sometimes random thoughts that can debilitate. By proactively choosing the right words and actions, some people overcome those morning limitations set by the mind. They have certain rituals. A morning run, meditation, prayer or their morning cup of coffee while walking the dog. Why Jermaine? He understands everyone gets 24 hours a day. It's about what you're doing with your 24. He fights the overthinking mind each day. He has a clear purpose. He is a person that has a crystal-clear objective - to provide for his children more than he had growing up or to successfully launch their business. Whatever their cause, he has a magnet attracting them to their goals.

Why Jermaine? He accepts imperfection. He doesn't say, "It's not a good time right now." He does say, "It's always a good time right here and right now." He knows the right time will never come. You have to go out and make it the right time.

Why Jermaine? He doesn't gossip or pay attention to the critics. People like him don't get distracted by the naysayers, doubters or haters. He doesn't allow the negativity to enter his mind. Shrugging off a desire to gossip or respond to critics, people like Jermaine smile and keep walking forward.

Jermaine feels more than he thinks. He is often driven by emotion and passion about his endeavor. Thinking is important and he does think...lol but too often we only let our mind direct us forward, and when we face difficult circumstance, we are conflicted between what we think and what we feel. Why Jermaine? People like him seem to lead from the heart, not the head.

He focuses on the goal, not the plan. Plans can change. Chaos can interrupt the best laid plans, but his goal remains the same. A happy relationship, talented kids, meaningful work and a successful career -- these usually remain constant, but how we get there can change over time. So Why Jermaine? He stays focused. People like Jermaine take lots of action. He has a way of trying things, even if he may fail.

Why Jermaine? He's open to meeting anyone, anytime. Jermaine engages everyone, talking openly to anyone who'll listen to his thoughts or ideas, opening their minds to change. Jermaine remains in the day to day, letting go of the past, and focusing on the present moments; he directs his effort at what he can control right here and right now. He doesn't worry as much about yesterday or tomorrow.

He believes in himself. Jermaine feels that all of us have this inner strength, this resiliency of the human mind, that can achieve great things. He knows that getting to success is never a straight line, but a path full of curves and side roads.

Why Jermaine? He's grateful, recognizing that life is not a right, but a gift.

Why Jermaine? He admits that he's not that smartest, or the sharpest tool in the shed...lol but he knows he can become smart and learn by trying. He recognizes that happiness and success in life comes from constant learning; he speaks about this when he tells his story.

Why Jermaine? He serves others. Everything from launching a new business to sustaining a happy marriage requires serving someone other than himself. He gives generously to others through his effort in his jobs, careers, business and his personal life. So if you ask me Why Jermaine? Simply because he is who he is - a caring, thoughtful, gentle man that wants to see people get ahead.

Why Jermaine?

Anjinette Hudson
Author, Poet, CEO, Screenwriter

I was privy to see the integrity, compassion, and character of Jermaine Jones before I ever knew his name. How?...I worked inside of Newark Penn Station in Newark, New Jersey which has quite a population of homeless individuals. I noticed Jermaine always smiling, as well as making those around him smile from a distance. This smile and light that transported all of those in his presence was truly infectious. As I spent hours, at least 8, inside of this station, I noticed the dim clouds of despair lifted weekly by his presence within in the station. Jermaine spoke to the hungry hearts of the residents of the station and offered them a meal. Speaking to people that many others have given up on, and that most forget, are still human beings. Jermaine always spoke to everyone with the utmost respect. He nurtured their spirits with his electric personality, compassion and empathy, as well as, nurturing their bodies with food.

As a writer and observer, naturally this experience was inspirational for me, as well as those he interacted with inside of the station on a weekly basis. On a weekly basis, I received confirmation that we all can make a difference because I was watching one man make a difference right before my own eyes. To witness humanity at its best was a great way for me to describe this weekly occurrence. Making a difference, like the name of his non-profit, is synonymous with the impact that I had become acquainted with before an actual introduction. The most genuine and honest impression isn't always the first impression, but to truly witness what one stands for before you know their name, is to truly know that individual.

It took almost 3 months for me to meet Jermaine face to face, and it was as much of a pleasure then, as it is today. Remembering the handshake and smile that I watched from afar, and that I finally received, was rewarding and only the beginning. The homeless and hungry within the station weren't the only people being gifted by Mr. Jones, because so was I.

I was gifted with bearing witness to someone truly making a difference in an environment full of the forgotten. From unknown to me, to a mentor to me, Jermaine Jones is an inspiration to myself and everyone who meets him. In almost 5 years of knowing Jermaine Jones, I answer the question why Jermaine with his character, heart, compassion, integrity, and personality are only the beginning of why Jermaine.

Jermaine is authentically who he is, at all times, even when no one is watching, or those that are watching, that he doesn't even notice. In closing, the world needs his high fives, firm handshakes, wise inspirational words, compassionate heart, and of course the present of his presence is simply "why Jermaine!"

Why Jermaine?

Denise Tolbert

My first encounter with Bro. Jermaine was at Christ Temple Church Ministries where I was blessed to be his pastor for 11 years before passing the mantle of pastoring on to one of my mentees. From day 1, Bro. Jermaine was humble and very respectful, but from my observations at the time, I sensed that he was in search for something greater. I've had the pleasure of watching Bro. Jermaine grow and develop into this determined and focused individual that refused to stop until he reached his goal.

I always knew, without a doubt, there was greatness in Bro. Jermaine, but he had to come to a point in life where he believed more in himself than what people were saying, and what life, and situations at the time, was dictating to him.

I have supported Jermaine from Day 1. No one is perfect! Everyone needs someone to believe in them no matter how many times they fall or mess up. It is my honor and pleasure to support him in all the great and positive things he is doing to help make our communities better. I love and appreciate Jermaine for all the sacrifices he has made on the behalf of others.

It has been my joy to be a constant in Jermaine's life. I have made myself available to him and his family for biblical advice, support, counsel, friend/mentorship etc.

whether far or near, he knows I am just a phone call or text away.

Everyone's journey is different. There may be some similarities, and there may also be different circumstances and situations that dictate the path of our life.

The best advice for someone on a similar path, based on my observations of Jermaine's life, would be to have strong faith in God; great determination; be self- motivated; be focused and surround yourself with people who are where you are trying to go. One should remain teachable and coachable.

I've learned from Jermaine that as long as there is breath in your body, you always have the opportunity to rewrite the script. Learn from your past mistakes. Pay it forward and give back by taking time to mentor others.

Why Jermaine?

Karen Trais

I met Jermaine Jones around seven years ago on a train ride from Boston to New York when Jermaine was the Conductor on my route. As Jermaine made his way through the aisles checking tickets, he seemed to have a cheerful word for every passenger. I noticed how the mood of each traveler, including my own, changed as Jermaine passed through the car. Again, and again, with each stop I watched him exude more than just an extroverted cheerfulness, but a joy. When I ran into Jermaine in the café car, I couldn't help but approach him and ask him about what made him so positive and spirited. Jermaine seemed eager to engage and was so open. He told me that had gone through some difficult times but prayed that his life would turn around. He also changed his attitude and how he approached the world, filling his thoughts with gratitude instead of despair. And his life did change. Even his family was astounded and puzzled by this new exuberant Jermaine.

Between performing his duties, Jermaine stood by my seat, and we continued our conversation. As part of his change in outlook, he decided to reach out to others. He related how he tried to be available for children in his community, those who needed a caring adult in their lives. He proudly unfolded a letter he had recently received. It was from a young man who had just enlisted in the army, telling Jermaine how much his help and concern had meant. Jermaine believed that just one adult showing a deep interest could change a child's life. This belief motivated Jermaine and others in his community to start Brothers Making a Difference. What made the description of his group so captivating to me was that the Brothers spent time just hanging out with the children. They took them to movies, bowling, or out for pizza. He also clearly enjoyed the children. So many children just see themselves as problems that it is astounding to them that adults can also take pleasure in their existence - and just have fun with them. Watching his mentees flourish fed Jermaine's inner joy.

That day on the train, Jermaine helped me see the value in my own profession as a social worker. I secretly wished I could do something monumental to change the world, more than just helping one individual at a time. But Jermaine helped me see that being a consistent caring presence in another person's life was also a way of profoundly changing the world.

During the course of that ride, we discussed our families, our spiritual beliefs and outlooks on life. We discovered that we had so many similarities, despite being from different backgrounds and leading very different lives. We didn't want our dialog to end, so we agreed to exchange emails. Through the years, Jermaine and I have stayed in touch, although I have not seen him since our first encounter. Jermaine thoughtfully sent me some Conductor hats and coloring pages to the delight of my then train-crazy 3 year old grandson. I wrote him back and sent a donation to Brothers Making a Difference.

Whenever I sent something, I would get a personal note of thanks. And our notes back and forth became more detailed and were a way of updating each other on our lives.

Jermaine also shared some of the other letters and testimonials he received from people who appreciated his tireless volunteer work and the contributions of the Brothers. Jermaine's gift to bring positive energy to all who interact with him has grown and expanded. He often gives motivational talks to groups ranging from school children to business leaders. He tunes into the pain and struggle each of us has trying to create a better life for ourselves and a better world. He offers hope and excites his listeners with the possibilities for change. I know my life is richer for knowing Jermaine, and I am eager to learn where his God-given gift will take him.

Why Jermaine?

Christopher Knighton

My first encounter with Jermaine was when he joined the church that I was a member of, Christ Temple Church Ministries. I was about 10-12 years old at the time and my parents had recently gotten divorced. He seemed like a very joyful, motivational, and genuine person. As I got to know Jermaine, I realized he was a selfless and supportive person. He always seemed to want to help people who may not have known they needed help. His organization "Brothers Making a Difference" was a great example of this. I made the decision to support Jermaine because I knew that it meant that I would be indirectly helping countless other lives that need support.

I would advise someone looking to follow a similar path to stay with God all the way; without the support of family and friends, it can seem that life may not have any purpose, so staying with God is important.

If given the opportunity, I would do it all over again. As a young kid, having the "Brothers Making a Difference" organization support me, and other young men at the church, helped me to see what difference it makes to see someone care about you. Knowing how that made me felt, makes me want to support other young brothers out there that may not have the support that they deserve through donation, teaching, outings, etc.

One thing I've learned from Jermaine that has impacted my outlook on life is to always keep it moving, enjoy life for the little things, don't hold on to negative feelings, stay rooted in God, enjoy the time with your family and friends, be positive around other people, and if you can, always try to help out someone. I'm now a senior at Rutgers University studying chemical engineering, and his outlook on life has helped me to appreciate what I have, strive to do better, and to work hard so that I can bless others with what I will have.

Why Jermaine?

Teresa Tolbert

My initial encounter with Jermaine was in the bowling alley. At the time, I had become a daily bowler and began braiding one of the other bowlers hair who said Jermaine wanted his daughter's hair done. So, she introduced us at Garden State bowling alley and I began doing his daughter's hair. From that day, a friendship with him and his family was formed. Jermaine was always energetic and had such a big personality. He would always keep you laughing, encouraged, and your biggest cheerleader.

Whenever he walked into a room, you definitely knew he was there. The atmosphere was sure to change when he entered.

As time went on we developed a great friendship. I saw his 3 girls grow from infants to beautiful young ladies that they are today. Jermaine would always help where he could and encouraged those he came in contact. I saw him have the most positive attitude during employment transition. A situation others may not have survived, he made it through with an upbeat attitude. I invited Jermaine to church, and he just had the attitude of sharing. If he found something good, he was going to share it with everyone. With so many negative things in the world, when you find someone who is always trying to turn a negative into a positive, you can't help but support them. His love and desire to help children in and out of his community is contagious. Supporting him in his endeavors is easy when he supports you.

I would tell someone trying to go in this direction, despise not, small beginnings. Although the road may be tough, lonely, and look like a dead end, hold on. As I have seen with Jermaine, regardless of the doors that may close in your face and the people that don't believe in you, keep pressing on, knowing that the doors that Jesus is opening are way bigger, and better, than the ones closing. Jermaine has always given his testimony, and telling those who would listen, how good God has been to him.

If I had the opportunity to regain this friendship again, I would definitely do it. The positive people, whether they are there for a season, or a lifetime, it's always nice to have people around that are always on 100. I have learned from Jermaine to be who you are. Some people may love it and some may hate it, but don't allow others who don't know you, to put you in a box that wasn't built for you. Continue to trust God, and put him first, and watch what he does. It will truly be greater than you think.

Why Jermaine?

Tyrone Williams Jr.

As I reflect on the question of "Why Jermaine?" The answer is simple, "Attitude." I had the pleasure of meeting and working with Jermaine in the early 90's while working at Lennard & Associates Special Transportation (L.A.S.T.). I served as the Director of Vehicle Maintenance; Jermaine was a Van Driver. Jermaine is a unique individual. He reported for work each and every day with a positive attitude and a smile. Jermaine's positive attitude is/was quite infectious and could change the atmosphere of any room. Our work environment was not the most desirable, as we transported clientele that were addicted to heroin.

Although, most of society would write off this group of people, and not even consider them worthy of conversation, this would definitely not be the case for Jermaine. He made it a point to connect with the clients, get to know them, and befriend them. He was more than just the van driver, he was their friend, even considered extended family to some. Jermaine quickly became the most sought-after driver in the company, as many of the clients wanted to ride on Jermaine's van. Additionally, he was often asked to help out in the office to assist with special projects and assist with dispatch. While working at L.A.S.T. our friendship, and respect for each other grew, and continued to grow after we both pursued new job opportunities. Jermaine and I lost touch for a short period, but ran into one another in Panera in

Montclair. We caught up, exchanged contact information, and have kept in touch.

I have been a guest at Jermaine's Brother's Making a Difference events and followed his motivational speaking/inspirational events. Over the years I have watched Jermaine exemplify a "positive attitude." He continues to spread his message not only by what he says, but he demonstrates it by what he does, on a daily basis. I am fortunate to have Jermaine as a friend, and happy to be able to support him as he continues his journey.

In answering the question of "Why Jermaine?" I pose a question of my own "Why Not Jermaine?"

Why Jermaine?

Jeannette Laguna
School Social Worker

I am writing on behalf of the students and staff at Heywood Avenue School. Three years ago, I was referred to Mr. Jones by a friend who spoke very highly about Mr. Jones' work ethic and dedication to serving our community. Mr. Jones is no stranger to Heywood Ave School and has continued to support our school for many years. Mr.

Jones recently participated in our Middle School convocation during the Week of Respect, where he spoke with our middle school students about the importance of self-respect and how it connects to building positive relationships with others. Mr. Jones is all about supporting others and treating everyone with kindness and respect. He has such a natural talent for public speaking and connecting with an audience. I can say with confidence, from my observation and student and staff feedback, that when Mr. Jones is presenting in front of 20 or 200 people, everyone is not only listening, but feeling inspired by his words.

Each year at Heywood, Mr. Jones visits our school during the Week of Respect and on College Career Day. Mr. Jones has never denied an invitation to work with our school community, and we are thankful for his continuous support and guidance. Mr. Jones is not afraid to share with our young boys and girls about his personal journey and struggles to get where he is today. He leaves a lasting impression on our young audience through his real-life stories and motivates us all that we are capable of achieving our dreams. Through our school wide character education program, we focus on leadership, responsibility, and integrity. Mr. Jones shares all of these qualities and many more. He is a wonderful human being who wants nothing more than for everyone to achieve personal and professional growth. I am honored to have been asked to write a letter sharing my thoughts on someone is truly one of best people I know. In gratitude and appreciation for your continuous dedication and contribution to Heywood Ave School, we thank you.

Why Jermaine?

Bobby Williams

It all started October of 1994; I had just transferred from Airborne Express N.Y.C to their New Jersey location located in Elizabeth N.J. While working on the dock I encountered an individual talking a bit loud. That individual and I began giving each other dirty looks. Of course, being young with big egos the stare downs were very uncomfortable. As time moved on the individual who I wasn't sure of. And I'm sure that individual wasn't sure of me, ended up working on the company aircrafts together. No words were exchanged between these two men other than the dirty looks, eventually these two individuals had a formal introduction. From there a slow association began between Jermaine and me. Although I was cautious about Jermaine, there was something about Jermaine that I could relate to. There was one morning right before it was time to punch out from work. I observed Jermaine upset, and he had punched the glass out of the company van. I immediately approached Jermaine, I asked are you okay? Jermaine who was very emotional stated "My daughter had an asthma attack, and no one got the message too me."

There it was Jermaine was passionate about his daughter the same way that I was passionate about my kids. I told him get in my car I will take you wherever you need to go, to get to your daughter. From that point two associates became friends. Jermaine and I build a bond that took us through several business ventures while still maintaining a positive friendship. I've watched Jermaine growth on all levels. We even got laid off together. I was the one that told him Amtrak was hiring. When Jermaine got hired, he refused to be stagnant in one position. Jermaine started as a Redcap, and now he is one of the top Managers for Amtrak out of Penn Station New York.

Jermaine approached me nearly eight years ago with an Idea to start his own mentoring business. He said after doing Big Brothers and Sisters for so long he wanted to do more. I said (Jay) Jermaine you can do it. Jay said I'm going into this with no clue, but I will give it a chance, Are you in? I answered him yes. Due to my career moves as a Police Officer after a few years I slowed down with program. Jermaine continued with Brothers Making A Difference. That passion I observed in Jermaine never left. We fed the homeless weekly, visit schools and talk to the youth, assist troubled teens and always try to give some hope to the youth. Jermaine has built his own legacy by being a giver. Jermaine has shown me that believing in your passion and not being selfish is a gift. Even when you watch Jermaine on the floor at work he is going above and beyond to help people, He interacts with customers to assure they are able get what they need during their travels. Jermaine has not lost his passion for what he loves. Jermaine motivates people with his positive energy. Jermaine isn't just a friend; Jermaine is a hero. My question isn't Why Jermaine Jones, my question is Why not Jermaine Jones?

Why Jermaine?

Appolos Laurient

I met Jermaine Sunday, August 3, 2014 at Penn Station. As I walked through the main floor waiting for my gate to be announced, Jermaine Jones' voice projected throughout Penn Station to customers in a panic with such gracefulness. The voice of reassurance that filled the atmosphere would transform the most anxious person to be impervious to the crowded surroundings as peace ensues. My encounter that day has forever changed my experience through Jermaine's words of encouragement that simply ended with a great call to action to smile. Jermaine Jones is the person that leaders look to for a refill on mood and mindset fuel. My morning dilemmas that trailed me to Penn Station were resolved with Jermaine Jones' words without him even knowing.

Over time, Jermaine has embodied his favorite and my adopted favorite quote, "Consistency is Key!" Through time, Jermaine has been so consistent, I believe that he is for sure here on a greater mission. Jermaine Jones' love and passion for his community is so inspiring and moving. Supporting Jermaine not only feels natural, but it feels as though I am a part of his greater mission as well.

In order for someone to follow in Jermaine's path, one must understand who they are and why they exist. One must remain consistent in servitude and love for people. If given the opportunity, I would absolutely do it all over again! Meeting Jermaine Jones has definitely changed my life. I can't imagine a life without encountering a more consistent human being that I get the privilege to call friend.

The one thing I learned from Jermaine that has impacted my outlook on life the most is, "don't forget to smile. It costs you nothing."

Why Jermaine?

Steven J. Young

AVP Transportation Northeast

Amtrak

I don't recall the first time Jermaine and I crossed paths as we both have had long and diverse careers and probably crossed paths in Newark, or on board a train. My best memory, and when Jermaine stood out in my mind, was when he worked in NY Penn Station for Mike Gallagher. Jermaine was a station manager in NY and was working with the Ushers to board trains. His energy and personality not only impressed me, but I could see the customers liked him and responded to his energy. As I walked through the station, I always stopped and watched Jermaine perform his duties. I wished we could get more employees to mimic his behavior and his dedication to the customer. I would tell Mike Gallagher what a wonderful employee Jermaine was, and he should be proud he was on his team. I must say, I was surprised by Mike's reply, only saying to me, "yes, he's loud."

It wasn't until 2013, when stations in NY reported to me, did I understand Mike's comment. I read through the numerous letters of support for Jermaine which were way too many to count, and the few, and I mean few, complaints all of stated he yells at us. I received my first letter of complaint in 2014, and as required, had to sit down with Jermaine to discuss it. It was this meeting that made me think, "what am I doing, this employee is outstanding." I showed Jermaine the letter and as he read it, I could see the disappointment in his eyes, he began to try and explain himself, and I stopped him. I said I felt I had an obligation to show him this letter and told him as long as he worked for me, he'd never see another one. I told him he has thousands of letters of support, and only a few of these complaints. I have watched him work over the years, and not only would I not change one thing he does, I would try and make more employees model his behavior. I told him at that meeting to continue the job as he always has and don't worry about anything else, I'll deal with that.

My support for Jermaine only grew over the years - his dedication, high spirit and energy made the busiest terminal in the US, a little less scary for hundreds, if not thousands, of customers. I was happy and proud to see Jermaine work. I have nothing but respect for him.

To employees who would want to follow Jermaine's lead I would say, be yourself, don't try to act but be your true self. I think that's the key to Jermaine's success. I take great pride in walking through Penn Station today when Jermaine is working and addressing our customers. He always introduces me to the customers as his boss and they always respond, you have a great employee here. I'd like to take credit for that, but that's 100% Jermaine. I will take a little credit for supporting him and always telling him "great job, keep it up."

Amtrak would be a better place if more employees, including myself, had Jermaine's upbeat and positive attitude. My hat's off to him on his journey to write his book. Good luck my friend and keep up the good work.

Why Jermaine?

Jermaine Hill, MA

I initially met Jermaine while working a midnight shift at Penn Station in Newark, NJ. I believe, at the time, Jermaine also worked a steady midnight shift for Amtrak. The environment of Penn Station during overnight hours can be adverse at times. Along with commuters present with intent to travel to different locations, Penn Station unfortunately also has population of men and women that are less fortunate. The men and women who endure this circumstance battle with many challenges such as mental health and substance abuse. These are some of the underlying realities that also lead to the criminality that exists in Penn Station.

Part of my responsibilities at my job is to secure NJ Transit rail stations, to include Penn Station Newark, from all criminality to ensure the safety for everyone while they are utilizing NJ Transit stations for traveling purposes. In order to achieve this I have to always be aware of my surroundings. One of the benefits in being observant is that it awards me the opportunity to make acquaintances with many people to include employees that work at Penn Station. I remember first observing Jermaine's character, and how he was always full of positive energy throughout the night, into the early morning, while performing his duties for Amtrak. His spirit was always very uplifting and his positive approach towards his work was inspiring. I learned that we had similar backgrounds and approaches towards life, such as overcoming challenges in life and continuing to persevere, and never giving up. In talking with Jermaine, I was enlightened that he was also involved with community service organizations, such as Big Brother/Big Sister, where he was a mentor and inspiration to our youth. Jermaine and I would talk about the importance of giving back to our communities, particularly our youth, understanding how important the youth is to our future. We would also talk about different ideas on how to uplift the less fortunate, and people in general.

I remember Jermaine mentioning to me one day that he wanted to start his own community service organization. It was not long after that conversation that Jermaine turned that goal into a reality. That reality became known as Brothers Making a Difference (BMAD).

I always say you can learn about someone by watching how they conduct themselves when they have no reason to believe someone is watching them. Ever since I first met Jermaine, I would watch him. I would watch how he approached work, how he interacted with many different people and I would also pay close attention to Jermaine when he was interacting with me. I am proud to say that what I observed was that Jermaine always conducted himself in the same manner no matter the person. He was always consistent with his energy and never seemed to lose focus of his goals. I watched Jermaine turn many ideas into reality. I also watched

Jermaine transform life experience and encounters into opportunities.

BMAD is a statement of principles that we all as men should wear with honor - being humble, while continuing to seek enlightenment and add to our purpose in life. Most importantly, it represents reaching back and helping another, and another, to believe in themselves and achieve greatness.

I am passionate about helping and being part of something at the grass roots phase. Jermaine afforded me the opportunity to be a part of the process of creating that vision for BMAD, as well as the vision he created for himself, through goals he set professionally. I've watched Jermaine rise through the ranks within Amtrak, as well as grow BMAD into a premier community service based organization and continue to embark on a rewarding journey in public speaking. There is a sense of pride and admiration I have always had for Jermaine. I always looked at Jermaine as someone who can brighten the mood of anyone he meets because his personality is so full of life and positive energy that it is contagious.

The advice I would give someone who is willing to follow a similar path as Jermaine's is:

It is important to be confident and self-aware. That virtue will allow one to believe that they can achieve anything, no matter the challenges.

Never be afraid to fail.

Life is a marathon not a sprint. The key is to keep moving forward. Set goals, but when setting goals set them with no ceiling.

Learn the principles of Emotional Intelligence. Begin to adopt those principles in your everyday life.

Invest in yourself. You are really the only one that can let yourself down. Always keep yourself in a continued learning state and be humble.

Practice positive and effective habits.

My last advice would be to remember that you can achieve anything you want in your life. The only person that can stop you... IS YOU!

Given the opportunity to meet Jermaine and support everything he has done again, I would do it all over again, without thinking twice.

The one thing that I have learned from Jermaine that has impacted my life is to always be positive and be consistent with your positivity. Jermaine has mastered the art of being positive; he has a bright personality that can light up a room and demands everyone's attention. His captivating personality is one of his greatest qualities, and he understands the value of a first impression. The success that Jermaine has experienced has been earned and well deserved. I intend to always be a supporter of his journey.

Why Jermaine?

Tim Murphy

My initial encounter with Jermaine was inside of Penn Station. At the time, I was working as a baggageman and he was recently promoted to Station Manager.

Jermaine came in with the mindset that he wanted change; and in my mind, he wanted to fix things that weren't broken. For example, we are required to wear helmets as baggageman when we go down to the tracks to collect the bags off the train. While most helmets were yellow or white, I had an orange helmet on. When Jermaine noticed I was the only one with it on, he approached me and told me I need to get a yellow one like everyone else. I didn't like it and approached him about it later, asking him what was the big deal about me wearing an orange helmet. He told me that's not in the policy, and we are supposed to wear the proper color. I didn't like it. I changed the color of my helmet to the yellow one, but was really upset he made me change it.

My feelings in my relationship with Jermaine actually made a complete 360, as I wasn't upset with him anymore. We became friends as time went on and I realized the type of person I am, and I the type of person he was.

The reason I decided to support Jermaine was because I saw the vision in him, and I noticed a change in how he went about things in life. He brought a positive attitude towards the job, as well as me.

The advice I would give to someone looking to follow in Jermaine's path is to stay positive, no matter what, and make the best out of whatever job or situation that you are in at the time. Most importantly, don't give up or stay complacent.

Given the opportunity, I would most certainly do it again!

Why Jermaine?

Ron Shaich
Founder, Panera Bread

I met Jermaine through my very good friend, Garrett Harker. We were looking for someone to inspire our team at our Family Reunion—an all-hands conference that happens only every few years and is a centerpiece of our culture. Garrett had seen Jermaine speak and told me he was the most powerful speaker he had ever heard. Garrett was right. I was simply blown away by the power of Jermaine's 'voice.' He is raw and real and just gets up and does his thing with little fanfare. I was amazed how he captivated everyone. Even our top-level people, who have walked very different paths than Jermaine but certainly face their own challenges, were able to relate to him.

As I kept up on what Jermaine was up to through both Garrett and through emails, I found myself continually impressed with Jermaine's integrity, love and pure willingness to help others. I decided to support Jermaine because he truly makes a difference.

You need to be honest with yourself on how tough it really is to move people in such an intense way. You must ensure you have the capabilities to succeed and the desire to help people, expecting nothing in return. You must have unstoppable will.

One thing I've learned from Jermaine that has impacted my outlook on life is that positivity often needs to be refreshed as life knocks us down. Never give up. Never.

Why Jermaine?

Amy Pozmantier

This is so exciting :-) One of the things I most love about you is that you give everything your all. You fill the room with your energy and passion and seek to help and share your story with every student - not just the ones who are easy to talk to or who are initially willing to listen. We have had over 200 different panelists in the six years we've hosted Career Day, and you stand out to me as a panelist that is a "must invite" - someone who NEEDS to come every year because he makes our school community so much better.

Why Jermaine?

Sue Sedivec

I first met Jermaine when he attended our Billy Nash Celebrity Golf Classic to benefit Big Brothers Big Sisters of Ocean County. He was invited to attend by Billy Nash (a former Little Brother many years ago), who by fate (I don't believe in coincidences), met Jermaine on a train. Billy was so excited about Jermaine attending and couldn't wait until we met. When I first met Jermaine, his full of life personality could be felt throughout the room. His warmth, compassion for life and outgoing personality made him stand apart from everyone. We connected immediately! He was truly a breath of fresh air. We didn't stop talking most of the night. He talked about the organization he was starting, and I shared about our agency. But more than that, he reignited my compassion for life.

Jermaine and I spoke frequently, and we met several times. Each time we talked, I was inspired by his positive outlooks to everything he came in contact with. This also changed my outlooks and my life. Jermaine is someone that you can trust, and he is always there for you, to celebrate your happiness and support you when things aren't going very well. Love this guy to the moon and back!

I was inspired by his dedication and determination to changing children's lives. I wanted to help him in any way that I could to start his organization and make a difference in the lives of the children he served. I also support him when he speaks to children and adults. He is a true motivational speaker. Once you meet him and listen to what he says, he will change your life.

To someone wanting to follow a similar path, believe in God, yourself and listen to your heart. Determination and compassion for what you believe in is also the key. Last but by no means least, be grateful!

If given the opportunity, I would do it all over again in a heartbeat! I love him!

One thing I've learned from Jermaine that has impacted my outlook on life is there is always a positive to everything, and you need to hold on to that through the good and challenging times. Never stop believing in yourself, and always follow your dreams.

Why Jermaine?

Tom Worstell

I first encountered this Amtrak Customer Service employee while waiting for my train on one of my trips traveling from Penn Station in New York City heading back home to Washington D.C. My train was scheduled to leave around 6:30 p.m. so I was waiting in the main concourse area in Penn Station for my train track number to be posted on the big board. I usually show up to Penn Station early and in this particular case, I was standing in an area in the middle of Penn Station next to the Amtrak Customer Service Desk located on one side of the main concourse. I always put my ear buds in and just attempt to tune everything out and listen to music while I wait for the train track assignment to be posted.

Anyway, this particular time, I kept seeing Amtrak customers approach this Amtrak Customer Service Desk employee with an angry look on their faces, but somehow, I noticed that each and every time, this Amtrak Customer Service employee turned every single angry customer around immediately. I saw three or four customers walk up to the desk looking very irritated and angry, but they each walked away from the Customer Service desk very happy, and in some cases laughing out loud. Their look while they each approached the desk initially would lead anyone to believe that they were each ready to rip someone's head off. Somehow, this Customer Service employee was quickly turning them around. After I saw this happen continuously, I decided that it was time for me to take my ear buds out and figure out how this Customer Service rep was consistently able to change the frame of mind of these very angry and irritated people.

At that point, with my ear buds out, I watched the Customer Service rep and listened to him as he stopped the next customer before she approached his desk and say, "before you ask me a question, would you allow me to ask you one first?".

The woman responded by saying "OK". The Amtrak Customer Service rep then said "how are you really feeling today, tell me the truth?". Then he said: "What can I do to make your day turn into the best day that you have ever had because we all need to be thankful for each and every single day that we are alive, right?". From there, the Customer Service rep then followed up by saying, "what can I do for you so everyone in this station can see that great beautiful smile of yours that you know you have"?

At that point, the woman smiled with the widest smile on her face. The next thing I knew, about 20 people that were in earshot of that same desk, started clapping and applauding her for her turnaround and big smile. I quickly realized that they also were all watching this Customer Service rep do his magic. It was at that point that I realized that I was not alone in recognizing this Customer Service rep's amazing skill set. He was already famous and had a huge following!

From then on, every trip through Penn Station, I purposely looked for this Customer Service rep and was always hoping that he would be working that day so I could enjoy the show each time! In most cases, I was lucky enough to catch him do his magic in many different ways. I started to really look forward to watching this "awesome motivational speaker" do his magic in the Amtrak station when I swung through Penn Station on my trips. On one of my trips, I finally got to the point where I felt compelled to go up and tell this Customer Service rep how amazingly shocked I was with his continual innate ability to have an awesome time at his job, while turning everyone's day into a brighter one as well. I just wanted to tell him how impressed I was and wanted to tell him to keep up the great work.

When I approached him, I was a little nervous about what question he may ask me as well as I approached the desk, but by this time he recognized me since I was one of his usual spectators on the sidelines that watched him each week as I waited for my train. At that point, while chatting with him, I asked him if he did motivational speaking or something along those lines. He responded by saying "yes, it just so happens that I do".

I immediately asked for his contact information because I was thinking as a change of pace, why not bring this guy into my NY sales office and have him speak to my team of 50 sales people to brighten up their day and provide them with some of this same motivation just to change it up a little. At that point, I now finally had his name and contact information. Jermaine Jones was his name. Over the next month or so, we exchanged emails multiple times and chatted a few times via phone as well. During that time, I got to know him very, very well, and in doing so, I found out that he was actually the Station Manager at Amtrak Penn Station, and not a Customer Service rep.

Anyway, we finally pinned down a date and time that worked for us where he could meet me at my lower Manhattan Sales Office to do a speech to 50 sales reps of ours. He was extremely flexible and did me a huge favor as it related to the speaking fee that he charged me. At that point, we were all set for the speaking engagement and I didn't want to ask him what his speech was going to include since I wanted it to be from the heart. I had faith in him based on what I saw him do in the Amtrak Station many times over.

With that said, I did prepare him a little by telling him why I was thinking that his positive attitude may help motivate our salespeople, and I explained to him what these sales reps do each and every day while they are in the office. I explained what types of obstacles they run into every day and expressed to him that they are told "no" many, many times throughout the day. I told him that if there was any way that he could help change their mindset after each time they are told "no", that would help them tremendously.

A few days before the scheduled meeting, we prepped some space in our sales office and had everything ready to go for the big day. I didn't tell my reps why I asked for an hour-long meeting with them, which was set for the following day. Like most salespeople, they were expecting another typical sales meeting of some sort, which usually includes some kind of announcement etc. etc. Little did they know, the legend Mr. JERMAINE JONES was coming in!

That morning Jermaine showed up early and he met me in our front office lobby dressed to the nines, with the shiniest shoes that I think I have ever seen as well! At that point, we took the elevator up to our office and walked into the large room where I had all of my sales reps waiting in their chairs. The room included an open area up front for Jermaine to stand and do his magic. I proceeded to introduce him as being an Amtrak Penn Station Manager that I met while waiting for one of my trains.

I asked him to explain to them what motivates him to do his tough job every single day. Two minutes into his speech, I looked around the room and noticed that every sales rep was completely engaged. His message seemed to be hitting home immediately with everyone in the room, just as I expected.

Jermaine went on to tell his personal, eye-opening story and as he weaved his way through the story, he mentioned some of the key points that he uses to interact successfully with angry customers at Penn Station. Here are a few of them:

"Going the extra mile is never crowded. If you are looking for no crowds, go the extra mile;" "Once you go the extra mile, you no longer want to do the bare minimum;" "Every time I go to work I tell myself, it's my first day on the job, this way I don't get too comfortable;" "Teamwork makes the dream work;" "Consistency is key;" "The only person you should be competing against tomorrow, is the person you are today".

Needless to say, Jermaine's speech to our sales team was a tremendous success and our sales reps continue to refer back to specific quotes from him when certain situations arise in the office.

I am very grateful to have met Jermaine almost two years ago now and to this day, we communicate at least once every two weeks or so, via text to stay in touch. Usually the exchange ends with one of his inspirational quotes that never get old. He is a great reminder to be the best you can be, every day and to enjoy every day.

Thank you again Jermaine! Keep up the great work!

Why Jermaine?

Noah Siegel

I first learned of Jermaine in preparation for a TEDx event in Boston, MA in April of 2019. I am the lead organizer of this event and had heard about Jermaine from Garrett Harker, owner of Eastern Standard Group. Before ever meeting Jermaine, I had heard about Garrett's serendipitous meeting with Jermaine at Penn Station in NY. He described a meeting where with one glance, Jermaine was able to identify deep emotions and instinctively help lift Garrett up. Essentially, Garrett assured me that Jermaine was beyond special and that I should 'take his word' that Jermaine would be a great speaker. Well, Garrett was right... In the months leading up to the TEDx event, I had many communications with Jermaine, all of which were positive, professional and exciting. When Jermaine and I finally met, indeed Jermaine was larger than life. It was natural to hug. It was not just any hug but a big bear hug, the kind reserved for loved ones. Jermaine's disposition and positivity were, and are, truly infectious. He fills every room with positive energy. It is almost impossible to have a negative thought when you are in his presence. Jermaine was a featured speaker at our TEDx event. We chose to close the program with Jermaine because there is NOBODY that can follow him on stage. From the moment he walked on the stage to speak, he owned it. The audience was riveted. Jermaine speaks with the perfect balance of passion, humor and emotional valence. He is a gifted orator, the likes of which I have never seen.

Jermaine's TEDx talk took us all on a journey and left us better human beings. The world would be a much better place if everyone had a person like Jermaine in their lives. Over the past year, I have had consistent communications with Jermaine via text. His communications continue to promote positivity, hard work, steadfast focus on goals and love. I question divine intervention when his text messages arrive at the perfect moments. I feel privileged to have gotten to know Jermaine. I am sure that there will be a time in my life when I will need support. In that moment, I will reach out to Jermaine. There is no question that Jermaine will be available to listen and lift me up. I hope that I can find the strength to support him, and others, in the same way.

Why Jermaine?

Rebecca Stein

Marketing Executive

I was traveling home to Boston from New York with my mother, who is generally a nervous traveler. The plan was to take the Amtrak Acela from Penn Station. Anyone who has been to Penn Station, knows it can feel chaotic and overwhelming trying to navigate the station thru the crowds and last-minute track assignments. To give my mother a sense of security, I approached a man in an Amtrak uniform and asked him a few questions about the best place to wait for our train. It was at this moment, Jermaine and his huge warm and contagious smile, entered my life!

Jermaine instinctually read the concern on my mom's face, and immediately created a calming presence in an otherwise frenzied atmosphere. A few minutes later, we were all talking about life, jobs, and kids! Jermaine saw to it that my mother and I received extra special care as we boarded the train, got assistance with our luggage and even found seats. We exchanged business cards and became fast friends.

From that point on, I never traveled thru Penn Station without spending time hanging out with Jermaine. Through regular email and text communication, I learned about Jermaine's amazing work with "Brothers Making A Difference." I also learned Jermaine was taking on speaking engagements at major companies and inspiring thousands of people through his life story.

Jermaine's impact on the many people he has touched, including myself, made me proud to recommend him to deliver the keynote speech at an annual leadership conference that I help organize. It was a great decision. Jermaine's energy, experiences and stories moved and motivated the employees who attended, from top executives, to managers and staff.

I have learned so much from Jermaine over the past several years. Most importantly, I have learned to treat everyone and every moment with warmth, kindness and importance.

I am so grateful to have stepped into Jermaine's path and become part of his inspiring story.

Why Jermaine?

Sylvia Veitia
Banking COO

I first met Jermaine at NYC Penn Station after our then in-house council urged me to go meet Jermaine in consideration to become our Annual Senior Management Keynote Speaker. Meeting Jermaine changed my perspective and appreciation for the power of positive thinking, and the drive that can be derived from such thinking.

Jermaine is a constant, loyal and inspirational leader. His consistent reminder and inspirational messages arrive at the most critical moments in my week, to ground me and stop just enough to appreciate the gifts and challenges my day brings. Jermaine's commitment to helping those in need is admirable, and his commitment is unequivocal. For those who are inspired by Jermaine's path - I would suggest you spend time learning from him, following his footsteps and simply spending time with him.

Meeting Jermaine has been one of life's highlights. He encompasses so much good, honesty, care and humanity that it is impossible to be in his presence and feel anything other than humbled and honored to be considered a friend.

Why Jermaine?

Brenda Walker
District Manager, Amtrak

Only someone who has not been fortunate to encounter him would ask who is Jermaine Jones. Jermaine Jones is an exemplary man. I recall when he was first hired at Amtrak, working as a baggage man. I would observe him going to the platforms early to aid passengers; addressing their questions and concerns, even though it was not in his job description. One day after watching him enthusiastically interact with passengers, I walked over to him and stated, "if this is who you truly are, then you will not stay a baggage man for long."

My prediction was true. Jermaine became a Zone 1 Conductor, then I hired him as an Assistant Station Manager for Newark Penn Station. Shortly after that, I promoted him to Station Manager at New York Penn Station.

Jermaine's ability to provide exceptional customer service and care to Amtrak passengers is undeniably remarkable. His huge smile and flamboyant voice are captivating. Over the years, Amtrak has received dozens of commendation letters, emails and calls from passengers expressing their sheer pleasure and gratitude from their encounters with Jermaine Jones.

He shares his life story and lessons to all that are willing to listen and learn. His life experience has made a humble, caring and strong-spirited man. He lives by example, and freely give kindness and love to all with ease and grace. It is truly a pleasure and blessing to know Jermaine Jones.

In his personal life, he is founder of a wonderful organization that offers support, guidance and genuine care to others. Brothers Making a Difference has helped so many people.

Jermaine, thank you for sharing your essence with humanity and planet Earth!

Why Jermaine?

Faith Alcantara

Principal

I am writing this on behalf of Mr. Jermaine Jones, President of Brothers Making a Difference. Mr. Jones has partnered with my school for the past five years serving as an excellent role model for our students. He willingly shares his personal experiences and outlook on life that serve as an example for others to emulate.

Mr. Jones has never turned down an invitation to speak to the students here at Heywood. He has served as a guest speaker/presenter at our yearly "Week of Respect" events as well as our "College and Career Day".

His delivery and message always gain the full attention and respect of my students. Mr. Jones' message is inspirational and leaves students with a sense of purpose and conviction to succeed.

I always appreciate the "nuggets of wisdom" he provides to our students. It is important to us that we engage our community and provide our students with opportunities to meet and learn from others as we prepare them for college and career readiness. Mr. Jones is one community member that I call upon year after year because he has proven to be an individual who connects with my students and truly has their best interest at heart.

Why Jermaine?

Nicole Graves – Watson, M.A.

Community Relations Specialist
Social Worker

Jermaine was cast out by society as an adolescent. Many thought he would either be incarcerated or dead, a common narrative that illustrates how Black men in America are disproportionately imprisoned and the effects of racial and economic disparities. Through faith, strong determination, the support of family and friends; Jermaine Jones turned his life around. After transforming his life; Jermaine reached out to help other young people; who were once like him. Kids that teachers and administrators labeled as "at risk". Kids that experience discrimination, miseducation and poverty. Jermaine embraces them and his words resonates with their struggles. Jermaine provides hope and exemplifies that they have the ability to overcome obstacles to reach their potential.

Why Jermaine?

Laura Toni-Holsinger
Executive Director
The United Way of Harrisonburg & Rockingham
County

At United Way of Harrisonburg and Rockingham County, we dreamed a few years ago of including a keynote speaker at our kickoff to Day of Caring, an annual community-wide service day. We threw around a lot of ideas and never really found what we were looking for. Then in February, my colleague Tashfia and I were traveling back from New York City after a conference and noticed this vibrant, larger-than-life person helping passengers in Penn Station get to where they needed to go. He exuded joy in his every move. I motioned to Tashfia, "watch this guy. He's something else!" When our track number was announced, we hurried over to line up to head down to board our train to Charlottesville. It was then that we witnessed the magic that is Jermaine Jones. In a matter of 10 minutes, we heard him say things like "Treat every day like your first day of work and everyone you meet like the CEO." After giving directions to one hurried passenger, he turned to those of us in line and jokingly said "I don't even work here. When people are lost, they'll take directions from anyone!" Needless to say, he made an impact on us on an afternoon that we expected to be a standard day of travel. On my way onto the train, as he was high fiving all of the passengers, I caught a glimpse of his nametag and quickly jotted down in my phone "Jermaine, Amtrak." I went home and Googled him and sure enough, I wasn't the first person to experience Jermaine! I reached out to him via the nonprofit he started, Brothers Making a

Difference and 6 months later, he inspired more than 600 members of our community who sat on their edge of their seats listening to his story.

The world needs more Jermaine's. After his visit to Harrisonburg, I have had many instances where I've found myself thinking poorly about someone or something. I then ask myself, "WWJD? (What Would Jermaine Do?)." It often changes things. Instead of seeing a failed community partnership as a set-back, I see it as an opportunity for education, encouragement and listening. Imagine if we all looked at life this way? Imagine if we all looked at each other as having this kind of potential? That is a place where I want my children to grow up and what I want my children to aspire to be. The power of a positive attitude. While I've always believed in this, it has always sounded so cliché. It's probably because I've never fully witnessed it or demonstrated it. I've been in jobs that were not my favorite, and I probably spent more time thinking about what I disliked than seeing the opportunities in front of me. I think about what Jermaine experienced and his willingness to take a job very low on the organizational chart, but do it with such pride and dignity. THIS is what it means to have a positive attitude and his trajectory is a prime example of what can happen for the good!

While he only mentioned it briefly in his talk, I also really empathized with Jermaine's experience of having a child in the hospital with complex medical issues. One of my children has a medical issue that came on very unexpectedly and requires life-long attention, changing many things about our lives that were previously not "normal." I know how this affects parents and have so much respect for those that have also had to deal with seeing their child suffer in the midst of their own life struggles, while needing to maintain a steady income. It can feel like the ultimate set-back. If we can summon strength in those situations, we can summon strength and positivity anywhere.

Why Jermaine?

Diann Coles

My initial encounter with Jermaine was when he came to New York to teach a class. The disposition of my mind was that of negativity. I had heard rumors that he was hard to get along with. My immediate thought was, "I can't wait to meet him. I hope he does come at me, so I can tell him a thing or two..." but as I listened to him speak, his words, his demeanor, he exuded nothing but confidence. I immediately fell in love with him; not in a romantic or biblical way, but as someone that I would want to mentor my son.

As our relationship grew over time, I'd come to respect him and admire him more and more each day. His personality is electrifying. I don't have to see him, but if I hear him, he makes me smile.

Based on these feelings, I will support him in any endeavor. He is a positive role model to young men and women all over the county. I am a woman of faith and watching his life, I believe him to be a man of faith. I believe God has His hand on his life and called him to do a particular service.

The advice I would give to someone who wanted to follow a similar path as Jermaine, is to simply speak with Jermaine. Given the opportunity, I most certainly would support Jermaine in whatever he sets out to accomplish.

The one thing that I've learned from Jermaine and has a profound impact on my outlook on life is to keep God first and stay positive. His energy is infectious!

Why Jermaine?

Timothy Greene
Special Agent

I first met Jermaine at a career day at a local public school in Newark, New Jersey. Jermaine was the same way that he is now - outgoing, engaged and prepared to inspire the youth. Jermaine explained his vision of how he wanted to give back to the community through his organization, Brothers Making A Difference, which was close to the same ideals that I held. Since that first meeting, Jermaine and I have worked together on various projects aimed at improving the community. We even came to the realization that we grew up near each other, as I lived in Newark, near the Irvington border where Jermaine lived.

Jermaine has become a go to person whenever I need someone to inspire the youth with one of his passionate presentations. I have called Jermaine at the last minute on several occasion after other speakers have cancelled, and Jermaine has always been able to change his schedule to meet with the kids. I have not met many that are as committed to improving this community as Jermaine has been. Although he has spoken to groups and organizations throughout the country, he still makes time to speak to small local groups without any fanfare.

I predict that the future is bright for Jermaine and that he will be the spark that leads a new generation.

Why Jermaine?

Bruce Broussard
CEO, Humana

It's hard to get lost today. Yet sometimes you need to get lost to find something you didn't expect. This happened to me a few months ago at New York's Penn Station.

I was traveling with my family, and we couldn't find our train. We were lost, running late and stressed. I was fortunate to meet Jermaine Jones from Amtrak, who stopped what he was doing to help. I could tell that Jermaine was someone who could write a book on customer service. Given how my company serves 14 million people, I'm always intrigued when I encounter someone who clearly loves helping people.

I certainly wasn't aware of Jermaine's title (I learned later that he is the Amtrak Station Manager for Penn Station), but it was obvious that he led by going above and beyond. I knew he'd be the perfect keynote speaker for my company's annual Perfect Experience Summit, a gathering of several thousand leaders who are there to discuss how we're going to deliver the perfect experience for our customers.

An inspirational story – that's still going on

Jermaine isn't a professional speaker. He speaks from faith, passion and pain. Jermaine is just someone who loves helping people and is in the middle of his own career journey. But he does have an inspiring story.

In 2009, Jermaine lost his job at DHL after 14 years, along with thousands of others. He didn't have a backup plan, because he never thought it would happen to him. With a wife and three daughters to support, it was very difficult, personally and financially, for him and his family.

Jermaine was at one of the lowest points of his life. Sitting in his back yard late one night in the rain, he made a promise to God that if he ever managed to change his mindset, he would never think the same way again. Jermaine picked himself up and found out through a friend that Amtrak was hiring. After 25 resume submissions by his wife (Jermaine joked that she wanted him out of the house), and a rejection, he was hired as a baggage handler.

Yet in four short years, mainly due to his new attitude, how his actions reflected it and leaders within Amtrak noticing his talent, Jermaine was promoted to Station Manager of New York Penn Station, easily one of Amtrak's busiest stations. He has been a Station Manager in New York Penn Station for four years and has been at Amtrak a total of seven years and six months.

Jermaine even managed to start Brothers Making a Difference, an all-volunteer-based "nonprofit organization aimed at enriching the lives of youth academically, culturally and professionally." He has run it for nearly six years.

Five lessons in leadership – regardless of industry

Jermaine did not disappoint and delivered an inspiring and timeless message to our leaders. Some highlights:

Going the extra mile is never crowded. If you are looking for no traffic, go the extra mile. Given my experience with Jermaine, it's clear that he goes the extra mile for the customer. As leaders, we should strive to deliver a perfect experience and inspire others to do the same. It's often the small stuff that turns out to be the big stuff in positively impacting someone's day.

Don't let the people change you; you change the people. That's how you hold yourself accountable. Jermaine has a very outgoing, positive attitude, and when he first started his baggage job, some of his colleagues told him to calm down. Jermaine felt that people sometimes look to contaminate you. He knows that when you're serving your customers, you need to be true to yourself and set an example that can inspire others. Customers deserve the best you can offer them.

Hold yourself accountable, even when no one is watching. Jermaine told our leaders that he never thought that if he changed his way of thinking, his entire life would change. He chalks this up to accountability. He knew that he could pass the blame to others. Yet when he looked in the mirror, he knew he had to be accountable. It's always easy to blame others (we've all done it), but we owe ourselves more.

Your setbacks can become a setup for your comeback. 2009 was a challenging year for our country's economy. Yet Jermaine brought up a great point. We all get knocked down. Use it as a way to address your faults so you can succeed the next time. For Jermaine, the toughest job was changing his own mindset.

Treat everyone you meet like they are the CEO. Jermaine said that if you treat everyone you encounter as the CEO, you never have to change your behavior because it becomes a lifestyle. Regardless of where you stand in your organization, leadership is not defined by titles but by actions. Give your employees and customers the best service you can.

Jermaine says character is built when no one is watching. As leaders, we have a responsibility to provide the best service to our customers and the best leadership to inspire our teams. Both deserve nothing less. We must always give our best, especially when no one is watching.

In any career journey, you will have success and failure. It's important to learn how to stay the course. But don't forget that getting lost can have its advantages, like it did for me that day in Penn Station.

Made in the USA
Columbia, SC
01 September 2020